CAUSES OF FAILURE IN PERFORMANCE APPRAISAL AND SUPERVISION

Recent Titles from Quorum Books

JOE BAKER, JR.

CAUSES OF FAILURE IN PERFORMANCE APPRAISAL AND SUPERVISION

A Guide to Analysis and Evaluation for Human Resources Professionals

Q

QUORUM BOOKS
New York • Westport, Connecticut • London

Library of Congress Cataloging-in-Publication Data

Baker, Joe.
  Causes of failure in performance appraisal and supervision : a
guide to analysis and evaluation for human resources professionals /
Joe Baker, Jr.
     p.   cm.
  Bibliography: p.
  Includes index.
  ISBN 0–89930–348–X (lib. bdg. : alk. paper)
  1. Employees, Rating of.   I. Title.
HF5549.5.R3B325   1988
658.3′125—dc19   87–37571

British Library Cataloguing in Publication Data is available.

Library of Congress Catalog Card Number: 87–37571
ISBN: 0–89930–348–X

First published in 1988 by Quorum Books

Greenwood Press, Inc.
88 Post Road West, Westport, Connecticut 06881

Printed in the United States of America

The paper used in this book complies with the
Permanent Paper Standard issued by the National
Information Standards Organization (Z39.48–1984).

10 9 8 7 6 5 4 3 2 1

Contents

viii   Contents

Tables

Preface

It is my hope that this book will contribute to improving the design and operation of performance appraisal systems and supervision. I believe that this can best be done by including the basic sequential steps of supervision in our system designs, and taking positive action to insure that these steps are carried out and the objectives achieved. The intent of this book is to provide sound practical procedures for accomplishing these tasks.

I owe a debt of gratitude to a number of organizations and authorities in the field of appraisal and supervision who took the time to participate in tests of the material presented in this book. Their comments were extremely helpful in insuring that the material is both theoretically sound and practical. The comments provided by Dr. Robert O. Brinkerhoff, Dr. Dale M. Brethower, and Dr. Charles C. Warfield were invaluable. I owe a debt of gratitude to my son, Mark J. Baker, who read the book and made helpful suggestions for improvement. I owe a special thanks to my wife, Katherine B. Baker, for her endurance during the time I was writing the book.

CAUSES OF FAILURE IN PERFORMANCE APPRAISAL AND SUPERVISION

CHAPTER 1

Introduction

Several years ago business and academic leaders were warning that the biggest corporate waste in the United States was that of human resources. Such statements were based on the conclusion that most organizations relied primarily on longevity rather than performance as an ultimate criterion for advancement and rewards. Time was used as the measure of all things because of its impartial, unarguable application to all employees (Lopez, 1968b). Many organizations may have accepted seniority as the ultimate criterion only reluctantly, but did so because of a lack of confidence in the measurement of performance and to avoid conflict. In addition, unions have traditionally protected their membership by insisting on the use of seniority when making personnel decisions. If this practice resulted in lower efficiency, the increased costs were simply passed on to the consumer.

Today, U.S. employers and union leaders know that they must increase the productivity of their workers if they are to be competitive in the global marketplace (Fraser, 1984). While the urgency of this need has become generally accepted, the means of doing so are more elusive. The methods employed vary greatly in both structure and success. In general, efforts have been directed to raising the quality and quantity of the performance of selected groups of employees, and the lowering of operating costs. The most common measures have included quality control programs, Quality Circle programs, the introduction of new technologies, reducing the work force, and the much publicized and very painful negotiations to limit and even reduce wages (Levine, 1983). Many of these programs presume performance errors on the part of employees and provide procedures for detecting and correcting these errors.

For the most part, such programs have been established outside of the normal chain of supervision and have been directed at raising the performance of groups rather than individual employees. For example, a quality control program usually involves a separate quality control section which tests the items produced by other work groups. Although these efforts may have improved the performance and efficiency of groups, additional measures are needed within the chain of supervision to improve individual performance (Levine, 1983). Since most organizations have performance appraisal systems in place, improving individual performance need not require the introduction of costly new programs. All that is needed is to make the existing systems work better. To make them work better, organizations need a way of evaluating their systems on a continuing basis to determine what is and what is not working (Lopez, 1968c).

PURPOSE OF THIS BOOK

The primary emphasis of this book is to describe procedures that can be used by the personnel of organizations to identify discrepancies in the performance appraisal system designs, to determine if their systems are being carried out in practice, and to determine if the desired objectives are being achieved. But, the appraisal of performance is an integral part of most of the steps of supervision. Therefore, it was necessary to include procedures to evaluate the critical steps of supervision as well.

A major portion of this book is devoted to describing a comprehensive system design for performance appraisal. The intent is to include all of the actions that must be carried out by supervisors and employees that are necessary for the successful functioning of an appraisal system. This system design is then used to describe the evaluation procedures, and as a standard when identifying discrepancies in the system designs of organizations.

Chapter 2 provides a general discussion of the concept of evaluation. The evaluation procedures for a performance appraisal system are discussed in detail in Chapter 8. An organization can identify which supervisory processes are not working, determine why, and identify specific actions to correct discrepancies without unnecessary expenditures of time and resources. Chapters 9 and 10 provide procedures for evaluating the formal methods used to measure performance and the actual performance ratings given by supervisors.

Chapter 3 provides a comparison of different descriptions of a performance appraisal system, and a discussion of the basis for a practical system design. This practical system design is described in detail in Chapters 4 through 8.

Chapter 11 provides a list of staff responsibilities for system evaluation and discusses training and education needs.

DEFINITION OF TERMS

A great deal of confusion has been generated in the past when discussing performance appraisal systems because of a lack of clear definitions for the terms used. The terms "appraisal," "evaluation," "assessment," and "audit" are frequently used to mean the same things. To avoid confusion in this book one meaning has been assigned to each of these terms, and an effort has been made to use them consistently.

Evaluation is used as a general term to describe the process of comparing what is to be evaluated to some standard. The purpose of this comparison is to identify discrepancies in what is being evaluated. For example, the evaluation procedures provided in this book involve comparing the appraisal system of an organization to a comprehensive system design which includes all of the necessary parts for effective operation. A discrepancy in the system of the organization exists when any part of the comprehensive design (the standard) is not covered in writing in the documents of the organization.

Performance appraisal is a special form of evaluation involving a comparison of the observed performance of an employee with a performance standard which describes what the employee is expected to do in terms of behaviors and results.

A *performance appraisal system* is defined as a series of actions that are carried out in sequence by supervisors and employees to: (1) plan what employees are to do, (2) insure that employees understand what is expected of them, (3) assist employees to perform up to standard, and (4) provide information for making management decisions.

Assessment refers to the process of judging the potential of an employee or job applicant for future job assignments. It involves using criteria that have been identified and validated as predictive of future performance. These criteria might include: level of education, experience, seniority, demonstrated skills, test scores, and so forth. An assessment is made by determining the level of attainment of these criteria by the employee or job applicant in order to find the best qualified person. The assessment of potential is not considered to be a part of the appraisal system in this book because it does not involve comparing on-the-job performance with a performance standard. The assessment of potential is considered to be a part of the selection process for other management systems such as the promotion system, the career development system, and the hiring of new employees.

An *audit*, when used in the context of the appraisal system, refers to the process of determining if established policies and procedures are being followed. In this book the term audit is limited to an examination of the records produced by the system to determine if timely formal measures of performance are being completed by supervisors for all employees.

A *performance review or interview*, when used in the context of performance appraisal, refers to a formal or informal discussion between a supervisor and an employee about the level of the employee's performance.

WHO CAN USE THIS BOOK

The academic community is frequently accused of developing theories and models that have no practical value to organizations. On the other hand, managers and organizations are frequently accused of not using the solutions to critical problems that are developed by the academic community. The intent of this book is to provide theoretically sound and practical tools that are of value to both the academic community and the practitioner.

Personnel in Organizations

There is a continuing requirement in organizations to identify and find solutions to problems that interfere with the performance of the work force. This responsibility is shared by all managers and supervisors. The personnel department is expected to provide assistance and support. Managers and supervisors should find the description of the supervisory processes that make up the appraisal system very useful in carrying out their responsibilities. The members of the personnel department should also find the appraisal system design and evaluation procedures useful for identifying discrepancies in the design and operation of the system, and when identifying training activities to correct these discrepancies.

The personnel department may or may not be officially assigned the responsibility for evaluating the appraisal system and supervision. Nevertheless, someone in the department is usually expected to assist in carrying out these tasks. That person may be the director of human resources, personnel manager, manager of training, director of management development, or someone with a similar title. The intent of this book is to identify the specific tasks to be accomplished, and to provide the tools to accomplish them. These tools are summarized in tables and appendices that can be reproduced and used as checklists and training aides. The narrative portions provide additional information that can be used when communicating the system to others.

Consultants

Part of the business of the management consultant is to assist organizations to identify problems with appraisal systems and supervision, and provide programs designed to correct these problems. The system design and evaluation procedures are tools that can be used by the consultant in providing these services. They may also be used to anticipate specific training needs of organizations, and to design training activities to meet these needs. These services need not be limited to a specific part of the system for which training literature has already been published.

Use As a Textbook

This book can be used as a text in a number of courses that prepare students for positions of management. The performance appraisal system provides a structural framework for discussing the issues involved in the management of personnel and for integrating concepts of behavioral science, supervision, leadership, motivation, and communication. It also provides a way of relating these concepts to the work place.

The procedures for identifying the causes of failure described in this book provide an illustration of a method that can be used to evaluate other systems of organizations. Since system evaluation is a necessary task that has received very little attention in the past, knowledge of evaluation procedures should prove to be a valuable asset to students and to the organizations in which they work.

The student of management is typically exposed to a number of theories and concepts that are general in scope and can appear to be contradictory. Some are confusing, some will always be subject to hot debate, and some appear to have no practical application in the work place. Students are expected to assimilate them into a personal theory or concept of management that can be used in future job assignments. At some point, the student must translate his or her personal theory into specific behaviors. Without some structural frame of reference or prior experience, the student may have a very difficult time accomplishing these tasks in the educational environment. In addition to providing students with tools that will be needed for future assignments, the comprehensive system design presented in this book can be used by the student to organize and integrate existing knowledge and to relate it to the work place.

USE OF REFERENCES

The references listed with each chapter of this book are intended as supplementary reading. Where possible, original sources have been selected rather than later publications that summarize the same information. The references are not intended as an exhaustive review of the literature. The primary concern is to provide a list of published material that provides information on the structure of an appraisal system. The emphasis is on what is done rather than how it should be done.

There are a number of books and articles in professional journals that offer detailed discussions on how each step of the process should be carried out. In addition, reviews of research findings and existing knowledge that have application to the supervisory process can be found in books and journals dealing with behavioral science, psychology, leadership, motivation, and supervision. It should be pointed out, however, that how each step of the process should be carried out may depend on a number of variables in each different situation.

SUMMARY

The logic of this book can be summarized in a few short statements. The performance of individual employees can be improved by improving performance appraisal and supervision. Organizations need a method of identifying ways to improve performance appraisal systems and supervision. The intent of this book is to provide a sound practical method of meeting this need.

REFERENCES

Fraser, D. (March 1984). Straight talk from a union leader. *Reader's Digest*, pp. 85–88.

Levine, H. Z. (1983). Consensus: Efforts to improve productivity. *Personnel*, *60*(1): 4–10.

Lopez, F. M. (1968a). Significance of the setting. In *Evaluating employee performance*. Chicago: Public Personnel Association, pp. 43–55.

Lopez, F. M. (1968b). Awareness and growth. In *Evaluating employee performance*. Chicago: Public Personnel Association, pp. 81–113.

Lopez, F. M. (1968c). Program review and renewal. In *Evaluating employee performance*. Chicago: Public Personnel Association, pp. 143–158.

CHAPTER 2

System Evaluation

While performance appraisal can be the most powerful tool that managers have for improving productivity, it is also capable of stirring strong feelings and conflict in the work place (Rendero, 1980). Because of this potential, a company's appraisal system is often allowed to function ineffectively, perhaps indefinitely, in order to avoid open conflict. The participants, including everyone in the organization, are likely to know that it is not working but do nothing to change it as long as conflict remains at a low level. As long as measures of performance produced by the system are not used for anything, most everyone simply ignores the problems. The benign neglect that often disables appraisal systems usually results in the elimination of critical supervisory steps or the permitting of supervisor processes to consistently fall short of their objectives. Supervisors may not complete annual or semiannual ratings for all employees. Those that are completed may be filed in the personnel records and seldom seen by anyone. Usually, other methods are used to identify and select personnel when personnel decisions are made. Getting promoted or receiving a pay raise may depend more on who a person knows than how much work he or she does. When it becomes evident that good performance ratings are of little importance, both the supervisors and employees lose faith in the appraisal system.

While some employees feel that personnel decisions should be based primarily on seniority, most believe that good performance should be recognized and rewarded. It is when managers and supervisors cannot justify controversial personnel decisions with valid and reliable measures of performance that disappointed expectations and conflict occurs. When this conflict becomes acute, line managers and supervisors usually go to the personnel department for help. It is at this point, when disruption has already occurred, that someone is charged with the responsibility of finding out what is wrong and doing something to fix the appraisal system. Line managers and supervisors may then be able to describe the symptoms, but it is the personnel department that will be asked to identify the illness and prescribe the treatment.

NEED FOR SYSTEM EVALUATION

The performance appraisal system and the effectiveness of supervision may be the most persistent problems of management. Managers are constantly bombarded with articles in the trade and professional literature that advise them of possible problems with their systems. Causes of failure are identified as faulty system design, lack of clear objectives, faulty supervision, and poor selection of measurement methods (Yager, 1981; Fournies, 1973). Other problems have been described for years and are reviewed on a regular basis. These include: difficulty in establishing what is to be measured, error introduced by the methods used, human error, and the shortcomings of the "traditional" performance review (Meyer, Kay, & French, 1965). Some of the more recent literature asks managers such questions as, "Are you complying with the Equal Employment Opportunity Commission (EEOC) Guidelines?" and "Will your performance appraisal system stand up in court?" (Holley & Field, 1982). Concern has also been expressed by agencies of the federal government that one of the causes of the lack of productivity of the American worker is the failure of appraisal systems and supervision (Mount, 1983).

Frequent changes are made in the methods used to measure performance; however, the symptoms of failure usually continue to exist because the true causes were not first identified. Unfortunately, the symptoms of failure can be the result of a number of different illnesses. For example, if a necessary supervisory process has been omitted from the system design or is not being carried out in practice, the system is not likely to produce valid and reliable measures of performance no matter what method is used.

Identifying the true causes of failure requires a complete evaluation of the system. If the causes of problems are not accurately identified, a great deal of time and effort can be spent without any visible results. The fact that there are so many possible causes of failure is a convincing argument for system evaluation. Nevertheless, it is one of the most neglected parts of appraisal and supervision.

WHAT ORGANIZATIONS NEED

A few years ago discussions were held with a number of personnel directors about the need for system evaluation. All of the directors indicated that they saw performance appraisal and supervision as persistent problems, and they agreed that evaluation was needed. But, initiation of an evaluation of "their system" was seen as a risk that they were reluctant to take. During these discussions, an evaluator from outside the organization was offered at no cost to assist them in evaluating their appraisal systems. The primary concern of the evaluator was to test a method of evaluation. The personnel directors were assured that their organizations would not be identified in the report of the tests, and that distribution of the results would be limited to them only.

All of the personnel directors agreed that system evaluation was needed, and each director gave serious consideration to participation, but all eventually declined. It was clear that the personnel directors had a number of concerns about the proposed evaluations. These included concern for the confidential nature of personnel records, fear of exposing discrepancies that were known to exist, and fear of conflict within the organization. One personnel director expressed concern that an evaluation might interfere with pending wage negotiations with the local union.

It was also clear that personnel directors were concerned with the use of an outside evaluator even though the service was free. Apparently, there was fear that the outside evaluator would expose discrepancies that they would prefer remained uncovered.

Although not given as a reason, the personnel directors were obviously reluctant to be the change agent for the appraisal system. The personnel department maintains the records, but all managers and supervisors are responsible for making the system work within their particular units of the organization. An evaluation would reveal how well managers and supervisors are carrying out these responsibilities. Therefore, the person who initiates an evaluation of the system may risk censure by his or her superiors and peers. One very effective way to reduce this personal risk is to assign the responsibility for system evaluation to a specific internal staff agency. Instead of a one-time evaluation effort initiated by a change agent, it would be a continuing responsibility of the agency to which it is assigned. Initiating a one-time effort, and carrying out a continuing responsibility assigned by top management, are two different things. In either case, however, the task must be carried out in a way that minimizes conflict within the organization. The effort must be directed to identifying the problems, providing assistance in solving these problems, and avoiding embarrassment to individuals and specific units of the organization.

Perhaps the major lesson learned from the discussions with personnel directors was that the proposed method of evaluation simply did not meet the needs of organizations. Organizations need a method that can be used by their own personnel on a continuing basis. An occasional evaluation using an outside evaluator is not likely to insure an effective appraisal system. An organization may run risks by evaluating its system, but even greater risks are run if the system is not evaluated on a continuing basis. A few of these risks are: (1) employees may not know what is expected of them, (2) appropriate actions may not be taken to correct poor performance, (3) the best qualified and most deserving personnel may not be selected for advancement and rewards, (4) valid and reliable measures of performance may not be produced by the system, (5) the organization may not have a defense when personnel decisions are challenged, and (6) the overall efficiency of the work force may decline.

TRADITIONAL EVALUATION METHODS

Although system evaluation has generally been neglected, occasional efforts have been reported in the professional literature. These efforts have used traditional methods which include: records audits to measure compliance, comparisons with the systems of other organizations, using some outside source of authority, and traditional research methods. Each of these methods, however, has some serious shortcomings when evaluating complex systems such as performance appraisal and supervision (Odiorne, 1972).

The first method, records audits to measure compliance, does not provide information about the "appropriateness" of policies and procedures. Further, it may not provide information about the soundness of the system design, the operation of those parts that are not recorded in the permanent records, or where the problem is if the system is not working effectively (McAfee, 1980).

The second method, comparing the system with those of other organizations, assumes that what works in these organizations will work equally well in the organization being evaluated. It also assumes that these other systems are in fact successful, and that they have been implemented exactly as indicated in the system design. It is unlikely that any of these assumptions are valid considering the differences in organizations, the complexity of appraisal systems and supervision, and the difficulty of fully implementing such systems. Portions of the systems of other organizations may be designed to meet local needs that do not exist in the organization being evaluated. These systems may include activities they say they practice, but that the bulk of their supervisors have never practiced. In short, using another organization's system design as a standard, and making judgments based on this comparison, may mean borrowing that organization's problems as well as their gains (Ordiorne, 1972).

The third method of evaluation, and perhaps the most common, has similar disadvantages. This method involves the use of some outside authority, such as a consultant, behavioral science findings, or a checklist published by an outside organization. The criteria used by these sources to judge the system have been developed by experiences in other organizations, are sometimes based on unproven concepts, and are usually general in scope. These criteria are normally reduced to a checklist or lists of questions that describe what the source of authority believes the system "should" be. In some cases the criteria describes the most popular concepts to make them more marketable, but they may not be the most valid ones. When using such checklists one can never be sure to what extent intuitive judgments, values, or even whims have displaced valid evaluation criteria. As ultimate criteria, they usually have many shortcomings (Brinkerhoff, 1980). Further, this method does not provide the structure needed for a continuing evaluation effort.

The last method of evaluation involves the use of traditional research techniques. These techniques typically focus on a limited portion of the system, and use experimental design and inferential statistics to examine the relationships between a few variables. Some researchers have studied the relationship between the accuracy of measures of performance and the characteristics of raters and ratees. Some have concentrated on comparing the accuracy of measurement using different types of rating forms. Others have limited their study to specific parts of the supervisory process, such as the effectiveness of the performance interview.

The problem with using traditional research methods is that only a small portion of the system can be evaluated at one time. It is difficult to isolate and study a part of the system in an organizational setting with any assurance that some extraneous variables, or unmeasured events in other parts of the system, have not strongly influenced the results and conclusions (Landy & Farr, 1980). This should not be interpreted as meaning that traditional research methods cannot be used effectively to evaluate specific parts of an appraisal system. However, their effectiveness is limited to those situations where the variables involved can be identified and either controlled or measured.

For several years, authorities in the field of evaluation have recognized that traditional evaluation methods simply do not provide the kinds of information needed to evaluate complex programs and systems. There is general agreement that what is needed are procedures that focus on a broad array of variables and provide the richest, though possibly not "scientifically conclusive," information possible. Information is needed that will permit a determination of whether a system achieves or does not achieve what it sets out to do, and to identify what is wrong if it is not working (Brinkerhoff, 1980; Provus, 1971).

A NEW APPROACH TO SYSTEM EVALUATION

In recent years, a number of methods have been developed for evaluating complex programs or systems. One of these methods, discrepancy evaluation, is particularly well suited for use in evaluating appraisal systems and supervision (Provus, 1971). This method can be described as a series of four steps:

1. Document and evaluate the system design.
2. Determine if the system is being implemented according to the design.
3. Determine if the objectives of each part of the system are being achieved.
4. Determine if the system is producing usable outputs.

Document and Evaluate the System Design

Documenting the system of an organization may require the consolidation of a number of different documents into one plan or system design. Portions of the system may be described in a personnel policies and procedures manual, a supervisor's handbook, an employee guide, or other published documents of an organization. It may be, however, that portions of the system are considered normal duties of a supervisor and are not written down anywhere. Once documented, the design can then be evaluated. The term "evaluation" in this context refers to the process of comparing the system design with a particular standard. This standard must be a system description that is both theoretically sound and practical, and one that identifies the supervisory processes that are necessary for the successful functioning of the system. The standard must identify what must be included in the system description of an organization. It should describe the actions that must be taken by supervisors and employees, what is to be accomplished by each of these actions, and what information is needed to carry them out.

When evaluating the system design of the organization, any part of the standard that is not covered in writing by the system description is a discrepancy. Discrepancies are then corrected by revising the system description of the organization. Once revised, it is used as the standard for evaluating system operation. If, however, major changes are made, it may be necessary to wait until they can be implemented before completing the last three steps of the evaluation process.

Determine If the System Is Being Implemented

The second step of the evaluation process is to determine if the policies and procedures described in the system design are being carried out by the personnel of the organization. This step in the evaluation process requires that information be collected about each of the actions that are to be carried out. The sources of this information are the personnel of the organization at all levels, and the permanent records produced by the system. If parts of the system are not being carried out, it is unlikely that the objectives of appraisal are being achieved. Therefore, it may be necessary to take corrective action before continuing with the next step of the evaluation process.

Determine If Objectives Are Being Achieved

The third step of the evaluation process is to determine if the objectives of the system are being achieved. The steps of the appraisal process must be carried out in sequence, and each objective achieved in turn, if the system is to function effectively. If an objective of one step is not achieved, the system breaks down at that point, and the steps that follow will not function effectively.

This step of the evaluation process requires that information be collected about each objective. The sources of this information are the managers, supervisors, and other employees. The information is collected by conducting personal interviews and using survey questionnaires. By carefully selecting the personnel to provide the information, a determination can be made as to which parts of the organization are having difficulty. Assistance can then be targeted at those parts that need it, and specific problems can be addressed, thereby minimizing the cost in time and resources needed to correct discrepancies.

Determine If the Products of the System Can Be Used

The final step of the evaluation process is to determine if the system is producing the desired outputs, and if these outputs meet the needs of the organization. The outputs of the system include formal measures of performance and information that can be used to improve the operation of the system.

Evaluation As a Part of the Appraisal System Design

Although the steps of system evaluation are carried out in sequence, it is usually possible to collect much of the information needed about the implementation of the system, and the degree that objectives are being achieved, at the same time. However, if there are discrepancies, it becomes necessary to make corrections before continuing the evaluation to determine if the changes create the desired effect. Changes in personnel and other factors may result in additional discrepancies in operation. Therefore, there is a continuing need for evaluation and updating if the system is to function effectively. To insure that the evaluation process runs smoothly, procedures to accomplish the necessary tasks on a continuing basis should be included in the system design of the organization.

SUMMARY

The intent of this chapter was to provide an overview of the need for system evaluation and a sound and practical evaluation method. An evaluation concept was described which included: (1) documenting and evaluating the system design, (2) determining if the system is being carried out in practice, (3) determining if the system objectives are being achieved, and (4) determining if the system is producing the desired outputs, and if they meet the needs of the organization.

In the chapters that follow a comprehensive appraisal system is described that can be used by organizations as a standard when evaluating appraisal systems. This system description also includes evaluation procedures that can be used by the personnel of an organization to evaluate their own appraisal system.

REFERENCES

Brinkerhoff, R. O. (1980). Evaluation of inservice programs. *Teacher Education and Special Education, 3*(3): 27–38.

Fournies, F. F. (1973). *Management performance appraisal: A national study.* Somerville, NJ: F. F. Fournies Associates.

Holley, W. H., Field, H. S., & Barnett, N. J. (1976). Analyzing performance appraisal systems: An empirical study. *Personnel Journal, 55*(September): 457–463.

Holley, W. H., & Field, H. S. (1982). Will your performance appraisal system hold up in court? *Personnel, 59*(1): 59–64.

Landy, F. J., & Farr, J. L. (1980). Performance rating. *Psychological Bulletin, 87*(1): 72–107.

Leonard, W. P. (1962). *The management audit: An appraisal of management methods and performance*. Englewood Cliffs, NJ: Prentice-Hall.

Macher, K. (1986). The politics of organizations. *Personnel Journal, 65*(February): 80–84.

McAfee, R. B. (1980). Evaluating the personnel department internal functions. *Personnel Journal, 57*(3): 56–62.

Meyer, H. H., Kay, K., & French, J. R. P., Jr. (1965). Split roles in performance appraisal. *Harvard Business Review, 43*(1): 123–129.

Mount, M. K. (1983). Comparisons of managerial and employee satisfaction with a performance appraisal system. *Personnel Psychology, 36*: 99–109.

Odiorne, G. S. (1972). Evaluating the personnel program. In J. J. Famularo (Ed.), *Handbook of modern personnel administration*. New York: McGraw-Hill, pp. 8–1 to 8–14.

Provus, M. (1971). *Discrepancy evaluation for education program improvement and assessment*. Berkeley, CA: McCutchan.

Rendero, T. (1980). Consensus: Performance appraisal practices. *Personnel, 57*(6): 4–12.

Romberg, R. V. (1986). Performance appraisal 1: Risks and rewards. *Personnel, 63*(8): 20–26.

Wadsworth, G. W., Jr. (1962). Seniority and merit ratings in labor relations. In T. L. Whisler & S. F. Harper (Eds.), *Performance appraisal research and practices*. New York: Holt, Rhinehart, & Winston, pp. 55–64.

Wehrenberg, S. B. (1986). The vicious circle of training and organizational development. *Personnel Journal, 65*(July): 94–100.

Worthen, B. R., & Sanders, J. R. (1973). *Education evaluation: Theory and practice*. Worthington, OH: Charles A. Jones, pp. 22–44.

Yager, E. (1981). A critique of performance appraisal systems. *Personnel Journal, 60*(February): 129–133.

CHAPTER 3

Performance Appraisal System Design

Many of the difficulties encountered by organizations with performance appraisal systems are the result of inadequate system design (Fournies, 1973). When asked to describe their performance appraisal system, most people reply that their system consists of some type of rating form that is completed for each employee annually or semiannually. Not mentioned are the many supervisory processes that are necessary for the successful functioning of the system. This is not surprising since the personnel policies and procedures of many organizations are limited to the annual or semiannual ratings. Furthermore, it is not easy to find a usable description of a performance appraisal system in the literature. Although we have gained a great deal of knowledge over the years about the supervisory process, we still have difficulty deciding which parts of supervision are parts of the appraisal system.

Though volumes have been written about the selection of the correct method for measuring performance, the human and measurement error associated with each method, and the interpretation of the data obtained from these measures, it is acknowledged that such measures are of questionable value unless a number of other supervisory processes are carried out effectively. For example, most everyone agrees that supervisors must ensure that employees know what is expected of them, observe and measure performance, and provide coaching and feedback if annual and semiannual ratings are to be useful, valid, and reliable. Some authorities, however, argue that these supervisory processes are not parts of the appraisal system (Yager, 1981). Others suggest that supervisors will be "encouraged" to carry out these processes because of the requirement to complete the annual and semiannual ratings (Wexley & Yukl, 1977). On the other hand, some supervisory processes may be considered parts of the appraisal system that are clearly parts of other human resource management systems. For example, the uses made of measures of performance by the promotion and pay systems are frequently discussed in the context of the appraisal system.

DIFFERENT CONCEPTS OF APPRAISAL

The different concepts of appraisal can be described in terms of the typical performance appraisal strategy. The typical strategy consists of the steps, or supervisory processes, listed below (McGregor, 1960).

1. Tell the employee what is expected of him or her.
2. Observe performance and provide feedback to the employee.
3. Complete a formal summary of performance at the end of specified period of time.
4. Conduct a formal performance interview or review.
5. Use the formal measures of performance to make personnel management decisions.

Most authorities agree that all of the steps of the strategy are necessary if the system is to function successfully. However, there is disagreement about which of these steps are parts of an appraisal system. In general, the system descriptions found in the literature can be classified as either summative or formative concepts.

Summative Concepts of Appraisal

The summative concepts of appraisal emphasize steps three through five of the typical appraisal strategy. Those who support summative concepts usually describe an appraisal system as consisting of the process of completing one of the standardized rating forms at the end of a specified period of time, conducting an interview or performance review, and using performance ratings to make personnel decisions. They recognize that steps one and two of the strategy are necessary parts of the supervisory process, but they do not include these steps in their descriptions of an appraisal system. They consider, however, that the requirement to complete a rating form at the end of the period will ''encourage'' supervisors to carry out steps one and two. The literature that describes the summative concepts usually places emphasis on identifying what is to be measured by the rating form, the psychometric properties of different rating methods, factors which result in human error, the conduct of the performance review, and the uses of measures of performance in making management decisions. Management by objective (MBO), which emphasizes steps one through four, is generally considered to be a management technique rather than a method of appraising performance (Wexley & Yukl, 1977).

Formative Concepts of Appraisal

The formative concepts of appraisal emphasize steps one through four of the typical strategy. They usually advocate the use of management by objective or goal-setting methods, and place less emphasis on producing measures of performance that can be used to make management decisions. In recent years, however, those who advocate the use of MBO and goal setting have recognized that these methods do not produce measures of performance that can be used for personnel management decisions. Therefore, they usually recommend that one of the standardized rating methods be used, in addition to MBO, to correct this shortcoming (Tosi & Carroll, 1970).

A PRACTICAL SYSTEM DESIGN

In actual practice, the arguments presented by the advocates of different concepts of appraisal seem more academic than real. What is needed is a single system description that is applicable to all organizations. If all of the supervisory processes of the typical appraisal strategy are necessary for the system to function successfully, then all of them must be included in an organization's description of its appraisal system. Based on this conclusion, the typical strategy provides a general outline for a practical appraisal system.

One of the most successful contemporary approaches to describing complex management systems is systems theory. The systems approach encourages taking a broader and more analytical look at familiar problems (Slusher, 1975). A system can be thought of as having inputs, processes, and outputs. Inputs are taken from outside of the system, changed by some process, and outputs are produced in the form of products or services. A general system design for performance appraisal can be generated using systems theory as shown in Table 1. The processes of the system are the first four steps of the typical appraisal strategy. The fifth step of the typical strategy (using measures of performance in making management decisions) is not included in Table 1 because it is clearly part of other management systems. A fifth process has been added to provide a structure for continuous system evaluation. A boundary is drawn around these five steps to establish the limits of the overall system. Also, each of the steps of the strategy becomes a subsystem of appraisal.

Processes

In Subsystem 1.0, the supervisor and the employee review the inputs to the appraisal system, and develop the standard to which the employee's performance will be compared during the work period. This standard is expressed in terms of the results (outcomes) that the employee is expected to achieve and the activities (behaviors) that the employee is expected to carry out. The results expected may be expressed as some quantity and quality of output, goals, and/or objectives.

In Subsystem 2.0, the supervisor observes and measures the performance, compares the performance with the standard, coaches the employee, and provides feedback to assist the employee in performing up to standard. The supervisor performs these tasks as frequently as necessary to provide the assistance needed

Table 1
A General System Design

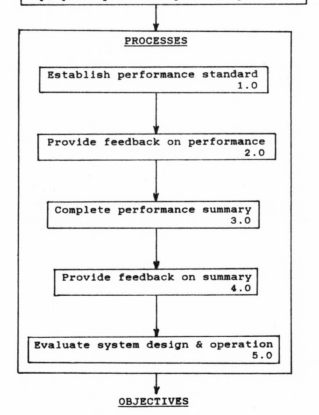

INPUTS

Philosophy, policies, procedures, rules
Job requirements
Expectations of supervisors and others
Formal methods of measuring performance
Employee's personality, ability, needs

PROCESSES

Establish performance standard
1.0

Provide feedback on performance
2.0

Complete performance summary
3.0

Provide feedback on summary
4.0

Evaluate system design & operation
5.0

OBJECTIVES

Measures of performance
Information to improve system

by the employee, and to make a fair judgment of the employee's performance during the period covered by the annual or semiannual performance rating.

In Subsystem 3.0, a summary of the employee's performance is made by the supervisor by completing a rating form. This summary should be based on the appraisals made and feedback given during the period covered by the summary.

Subsystem 4.0 is typically called the performance "review" or "interview." In this subsystem the supervisor informs the employee of the rating that he or she received for the period. The supervisor and employee may also discuss areas where performance can be improved.

Subsystem 5.0 has been added to the strategy to provide the structure for a continuous evaluation effort. The information provided by this subsystem is used to modify the inputs to the system. This might include revising policies and procedures, job requirements, methods of measuring performance, or the expectations held for the job. The precise identification of problems requires a methodical search, focused on the parts of the appraisal system in sequence, from department to department within the organization.

The solution to a specific problem may be to change the system, coach a few personnel, or provide a training program for all personnel. A continuing effort can identify specific needs, and target solutions to avoid unnecessary expenditures of time and resources. It should be pointed out, however, that the evaluation effort is designed to identify the problems. Actions to correct these problems are normally taken by other management systems.

System Inputs

An organization can be seen as a social system involving two major classes of phenomena that are independent yet interactive. The first of these classes encompasses the roles and expectations that will fulfill the goals of the organization. The second is the personalities, abilities, and needs of the individuals that work within the system. The organization defines the role that a job holder is expected to play by assigning rights and duties, and describing what he or she should do in a variety of circumstances. Roles may be formulated without reference to any particular individual and are interdependent in that each role derives its meaning from other related roles. But these roles are to be played by real flesh-and-blood people with their own unique patterns of needs and inclinations (Getzels & Guba, 1957).

Observed behavior can be explained as the result of individuals' attempts to adapt to an environment, composed of expectations held for their behavior, in ways that are consistent with their own independent patterns of needs. Failure to adjust to role expectations and/or to fulfill individual needs could result in organizational and individual conflict. In this conception of an organization, the expectations of the employee for need fulfillment can be considered inputs to the appraisal process, and also as inputs that, in part, define the role the organization expects the job incumbent to play.

As shown in Table 1, role expectations are established by: (1) company philosophy, procedures, rules, (2) job requirements, (3) the expectations of supervisors and others, and (4) what is measured on formal performance ratings. The expectations of the individual are defined by the personality, abilities, and needs of the employee (Lopez, 1968b).

System Objectives

There are basically two types of appraisal system objectives. One type is the objectives of each of the processes of the system. The second type is the outputs of the system. Each of the subsystems of appraisal are designed to produce objectives that are used as inputs by the subsystems that follow. For example, the objectives of the first subsystem are needed as inputs to the second subsystem. The objectives of the second subsystem are needed by the third subsystem, and so on. If the process of one subsystem is not being carried out or fails to achieve its objective, other subsystems are not likely to function effectively. Therefore, the objectives of each subsystem must be clearly identified and achieved to make the system work. When the system is not working, each of the subsystems must be evaluated to determine where the breakdown is occurring.

The overall objectives of the appraisal system are to produce the outputs shown in Table 1. They are: (1) formal measures of the performance of employees, and (2) information about how well the system is designed and working. Formal measures of performance are used as feedback to employees and as data by other management systems in making personnel decisions. Information produced by the evaluation subsystem is an output that is used to modify the inputs to the appraisal system to improve efficiency.

Whether or not these outputs of the appraisal system are available for use depends on the success of the efforts made to collect, store, retrieve, and analyze the information. If retrieval is difficult and time consuming, the use of the information may be limited to the review of the record of a single employee. In the case of formal measures of performance, use of the data is severely limited if it is simply filed in the personnel records of employees. If this is the case, persons who are considered for personnel actions may be limited to those who are nominated by managers and supervisors, and those who make applications. Some high performers who are fully qualified may be overlooked simply because they are not nominated. The use of computer files to store performance ratings permits the consideration of a larger pool of qualified personnel, and greatly facilitates the use of this information.

A COMPREHENSIVE SYSTEM DESIGN

Though the general system design shown in Table 1 identifies the major steps of appraisal, a more detailed analysis is necessary is the design is to be a practical tool for organizations. Each of these steps actually consists of a series of actions or processes that must be carried out by supervisors and employees. The author, with the cooperation of a number of authorities in the field of performance improvement and several large businesses, recently completed a study to identify these actions, and to develop and test a comprehensive system design.

The actions necessary to carry out each of the steps of the general design were identified from accepted knowledge and the supervisory processes that are commonly used in organizations. These actions were integrated into a system design using systems theory. The systems approach forced the planner to identify the specific processes of the system, and to identify the objectives and inputs for each process. The comprehensive design was then tested in the field. the participants in this test found that the design is a practical and useful tool for organizations. They found that it can be used as a standard for evaluating appraisal systems and for a number of other purposes. The test indicated that organizations can use the design to: (1) explain why appraisal is necessary and important, (2) develop training programs, (3) develop seminars for supervisors, (4) develop a manual to be used by company officers for evaluating the appraisal system in their departments, (5) think through an appraisal training design and communication process, (6) to develop management coaching programs, and (7) as a basic concept to evaluate other personnel systems.

The comprehensive appraisal system design is described in detail in Chapters 4 through 8 of this book. It provides the structure for an appraisal system, or what should be described in the policies and procedures of an organization. The primary focus is on what to do and why. "What" refers to the steps of the supervisory processes and the information needed to carry them out. "Why" refers to the objectives that are to be achieved.

Less emphasis has been placed on trying to explain "how" each of the supervisory processes should be carried out. How they should be carried out will vary with the task to be accomplished; the work environment; the personalities of the supervisor and employee; the leadership skills of the supervisor; the abilities, knowledge, skills, and needs of the employee; and other factors that may not yet be identified. Because of the interaction of these variables, how the processes of supervision should be carried out may vary in each situation. Further, they may be carried out differently by different supervisors but achieve the same results. For these reasons it may be impossible and undesirable to try to describe in organizational policies and procedures how each process should be carried out. Instead, it may be better to recognize that these variables exist, and design procedures that insure that they are properly considered in the process.

Finding out how something should be done is frequently the objective of researchers who formulate and test theories of leadership, motivation, supervision, psychology, and behavioral science. When they are successful, their findings may become common practice and may be incorporated into the appropriate systems of organizations. They then become "what is done," and part of the structure of the system.

SUMMARY

This chapter has provided a general outline of an appraisal system. However, a more detailed analysis must be made of each of the subsystems. Each subsystem actually consists of a series of actions that must be carried out by supervisors and their employees. In the chapters that follow, a more complete analysis is made of each subsystem to identify these actions, their objectives, and the information needed to carry them out. In making this deeper analysis, systems theory is used to integrate existing knowledge of supervision and the appraisal of human performance. An organization can use the detailed description as a standard to evaluate its system and as an outline for documenting its system design.

REFERENCES

Bernardin, H. J., & Klatt, L. A. (1985). Managerial appraisal systems: Has practice caught up to the state of the art? *Personnel Administrator, 30*(11): 79–86.

Echles, R. W., Carmichael, R. L., & Sarchet, B. R. (1974a). Counseling, giving orders, introducing change, and conducting meetings. In *Essentials of management for first-line supervisors*. New York: John Wiley & Sons, pp. 430–456.

Fournies, F. F. (1973). *Management performance appraisal: A national study*. Somerville, NJ: F. F. Fournies Associates.

Getzels, J. W., & Guba, E. G. (1957). Social behavior and the administrative process. *School Review, 65*(4): 423–441.

Gomez-Mejia, L. R., Page, R. C., & Tornov, W. W. (1985). Improving the effectiveness of performance appraisal. *Personnel Administrator, 30*(1): 74–80.

Haynes, M. G. (1978). Developing an appraisal program. *Personnel Journal, 57*(January): 14–19.

Lloyd, W. F., Jr. (1977). Performance appraisal: A shortsighted approach for installing a workable program. *Personnel Journal, 56*(September): 446–450.

Locker, A. H., & Teel, K. S. (1977). Performance appraisal: A survey of current practices. *Personnel Journal, 56*(September): 245–257.

Lopez, F. M. (1968a). Significance of the setting. In *Evaluating employee performance*. Chicago: Public Personnel Association, pp. 43–55.

Lopez, F. M. (1968b). Awareness and growth. In *Evaluating employee performance*. Chicago: Public Personnel Association, pp. 81–113.

McGregor, D. (1960). A critique of performance appraisal. In *The human side of enterprise*. New York: McGraw-Hill, pp. 77–89.

Slusher, E. A. (1975). A systems look at performance appraisal. *Personnel Journal, 54*(February): 114–117.

Teel, K. S. (1980). Performance appraisal: Current trends and persistent progress. *Personnel Journal, 59*(April): 296–301, 316.

Tosi, H. L., & Carroll, S. (1970). Management by objective. *Personnel Administrator, 33*(3): 44–48.

Wexley, K. N., & Yukl, G. A. (1977). Measuring employee proficiency. In *Organi-*

zational behavior and personnel psychology. Homewood, IL: Richard D. Irwin, Inc., pp. 197–228.

Yager, E. (1981). A critique of performance appraisal systems. *Personnel Journal, 60*(February): 129–133.

CHAPTER 4

Establishing the Performance Standard

The first step of the appraisal strategy is to identify what the employee is to do and what results he or she is to achieve. When these activities and results are identified they are used as a standard to which the on-the-job performance of the employee is compared. If the employee carries out the planned activities and achieves the planned results, his or her performance is judged to be up to standard.

In most organizations there are individuals that never seem to perform up to the standards expected of them. They may be fully qualified, capable people who are willing to do their best, but their efforts always seem to be short of the mark. Frequently, when their supervisor is replaced, a dramatic turnaround occurs. In many cases such changes are easily explained. The new supervisor simply does a better job of making sure that these individuals know what is expected of them.

It is the task of the supervisor and the employee to identify a performance standard that is within the capability of the employee and that will make the maximum contribution to the goals of the work unit. The supervisor is in the best position to identify what is necessary to achieve the goals of the work unit, while the employee usually has first-hand knowledge of the operational demands of his or her job. In addition, the employee is a primary source of information about his or her own aspirations and abilities (Getzels & Guba, 1957).

It is in the best interest of both the supervisor and the employee to set a performance standard that is neither too high or too low. If set too high, the employee is not likely to achieve the standard. If set too low, the employee's contribution may be judged as inadequate by others in the work unit and the organization. In either case, the goals of the work unit may not be achieved.

Unfortunately, some supervisors assume that job descriptions tell employee's what is expected of them. Supervisors may continue to make this false assumption even when it is clear that performance is being judged on a number of criteria that are not included in job descriptions. The end result is that both the supervisor and employee must identify what the true performance standard is through trial and error. The supervisor must decide on a day-to-day basis what he or she expects of the employees. The employees must judge their own performance on the basis of the job description, and learn what the true standard is by making mistakes and being corrected by the supervisor. Though it is important to learn from mistakes, unnecessary mistakes are costly and disruptive. Few things are more frustrating than being corrected for doing what you thought was right. Many mistakes can be avoided if the true performance standard is established at the start and adjusted during the cycle to account for new circumstances.

It is also in the best interest of both the supervisor and the employee to insure that there is a mutual understanding of what must be considered when establishing the performance standard, and what the standard is once it is established. There are four steps or processes that are considered necessary if this mutual under-standing is to be achieved. These processes are shown in Table 2. This table also shows the objectives and the inputs for each of the processes.

REVIEWING THE INPUTS TO APPRAISAL

In Process 1.1, Table 2, the supervisor and the employee exchange views on their understanding of the inputs to the appraisal system. The inputs are the sources of the information that is needed to establish the performance standard. The objective of this process is to develop a mutual understanding of how the other interprets the inputs. If there appears to be a lack of understanding or differences of opinion, the discussion is continued until the differences are re-solved. The employee must participate to the extent that there is effective com-munication and to the extent that he or she provides the information needed by the supervisor.

Misunderstandings and differences of perceptions can result if the supervisor simply assumes that the employee uses words in the same way that he or she does. The participation of the employee is necessary if such differences are to be identified and clarified. If distrust, suspicion, or strong uncertainty exists in the mind of the employee about the inputs to the system, openness will be discouraged. To the extent that employees understand the system and its uses, and see it as fair and objective, most will welcome the chance to participate.

Without this exchange, there is no way for the supervisor to know that the employee has received and understands the information included in the inputs to the system. The supervisor may be the only source for some of the information needed by the employee. Policies and procedures manuals may not be available to the employee and information from other sources may not have been accurately interpreted. Even if all of the sources of information are available to the em-ployee, there is no assurance that the information has been interpreted in the same way as the supervisor.

Table 2
Subsystem 1.0: Establish Performance Standard

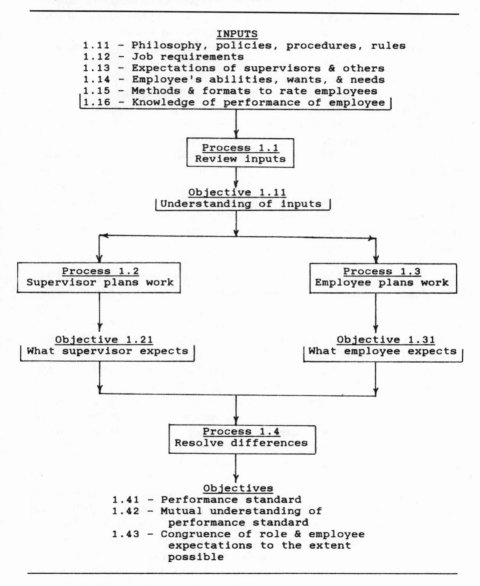

INPUTS
1.11 – Philosophy, policies, procedures, rules
1.12 – Job requirements
1.13 – Expectations of supervisors & others
1.14 – Employee's abilities, wants, & needs
1.15 – Methods & formats to rate employees
1.16 – Knowledge of performance of employee

Process 1.1
Review inputs

Objective 1.11
Understanding of inputs

Process 1.2
Supervisor plans work

Process 1.3
Employee plans work

Objective 1.21
What supervisor expects

Objective 1.31
What employee expects

Process 1.4
Resolve differences

Objectives
1.41 – Performance standard
1.42 – Mutual understanding of
       performance standard
1.43 – Congruence of role & employee
       expectations to the extent
       possible

System Inputs

The inputs to the appraisal system, listed in Table 2, include: (1) philosophy, policies, procedures, and rules of the organization; (2) the requirements of the job to which the employee is assigned; (3) the expectations for the person assigned the job that are held by different levels of management and supervision, by other members of the work group, and members of other work groups; (4) the employee's personality, ability, and needs; (5) the methods and rating forms used to formally measure the performance of the employee annually or semiannually; and (6) knowledge of previous levels of performance of the employee.

Philosophy, policies, procedures, and rules. Philosophy can be defined, in the context of an organization, as those enduring principles and values that determine objectives and the means of achieving objectives. Whether stated or unstated, every organization has a philosophy that applies with equal force and validity to all members of the organization. It may be disorganized, contradictory, and in conflict with the values of the social system, but it still remains the guiding spirit of the organization. On the other hand, it may be consistent, pervasive, inspiring, and reflect high ideals that instill a feeling of confidence between policy makers, supervisors, planners, and other employees (Lopez, 1968a). In either case, the philosophy of an organization must be considered when establishing performance standards.

Policies can be defined as statements of courses of action or lines of conduct that have been adopted as tangible expressions of the organization's underlying principles or philosophy. Procedures are usually intended to state how something should be done under normal conditions. The employees are expected to exercise good judgment in situations not covered by procedures. Rules are usually made to structure relationships, to reduce the need for continuous supervision, and to give security. Most organizations have rules in order for employees to understand the expectations of their positions, the limits of their authority, whom to report to, and who reports to them (Boles & Davenport, 1975a).

There may be other expectations that are based on, or are amplifications of, those already mentioned. These may be included in employee guides, supervisor's handbooks, program descriptions, and other documents published by an organization. The performance appraisal system, as defined in organizational documents, is an input to the appraisal process since it establishes role expectations for all employees in achieving the objectives of the system.

The development and transmission of policies, procedures, and rules for all conceivable contingencies that are likely to be faced by employees is difficult, and perhaps undesirable. Such directives could have such adverse effects as: taking away individual initiative, causing inefficiency, lowering morale, and reducing organizational flexibility. Further, no organizational planning can foresee all contingencies within its operations, anticipate with perfect accuracy all environmental changes, or control perfectly all human variables. Therefore, the resources of people in innovating, spontaneous cooperation, and protective and creative behavior are vital to an organization's survival and effectiveness (Getzels & Guba, 1957).

Job requirements. Job requirements (as used in Table 2) are defined as the duties, responsibilities, and authority assigned to a specific job. At lower levels of an organization the job requirements may establish rather specific behaviors that are expected of employees. At the managerial level job requirements may be more general in scope to permit managers to select from several different types of behavior. But, even when job requirements establish specific behaviors, they do not define them to the extent that all individual latitude is eliminated (Boles & Davenport, 1975a).

The manager, supervisor, industrial engineer, and/or job analyst divides the tasks assigned to a work group into specific job assignments. This is usually done without considering the specific individuals that will fill the jobs. The traditional approach to job design is to break the work down into small, repetitive tasks which are performed by individual employees. However, because job enrichment has become an increasingly important theme in recent years, alternative assignment methods have become common.

Job enrichment involves having each employee perform all of the tasks of a particular work cycle. The purpose is to eliminate the undesirable characteristics of the highly repetitive, specialized job. Job enrichment techniques include: (1) the combining of several jobs that require a wide variety of skills; (2) giving each employee a start-to-finish work unit through which he or she can have the satisfaction of completing a meaningful task; (3) allocating employees more responsibility for quality control and the authority to make decisions about work procedures; (4) allowing personnel to deal directly with clients, support personnel, and persons performing related jobs; and (5) providing channels of performance feedback so employees can self-monitor and adjust their own behaviors. These measures are not limited to enriching the jobs of individuals but are also used at work group levels (Schoderbek & Reif, 1969).

Some motivation theorists have argued that job enrichment increases commitment and satisfaction as well as the productivity of the employee. It is also argued that these benefits are strongest for those individuals who have high needs for achievement and personal growth (Herzberg, 1968). There have also been criticisms of the job enrichment approach. Some studies have suggested that the benefits of job enrichment are weak. In general, these findings suggest that while some attitudes may be improved, there is less impact on productivity. Other research has suggested that a worker's motivation may be a result of how one's co-workers see the job rather than the task characteristics themselves. One study found that both job satisfaction and productivity were significantly affected by social cues but largely unaffected by job enrichment (White & Mitchell, 1979). Although job enrichment is a promising approach for motivating and improving employee performance, it is not effective with all employees, and is inappropriate for some kinds of jobs.

The job requirements are usually detailed in writing in some standard format.

At the managerial or supervisory level the requirements may be broadly stated. Organizations that use the management by objective method phrase job requirements as a number of objectives and specific actions to achieve these objectives. For employees below the supervisory level, job requirements are often stated in specific terms in a job description (Boles & Davenport, 1975a).

Some authorities suggest that the typical job description causes problems even for receptive, hourly rated jobs, and that they are clearly inappropriate for managerial positions. They suggest that jobs are made up of a formidable array of activities that are rarely written down anywhere. Workers and their bosses often have different perceptions of what these activities are and which activities should be given priority. Job descriptions are quickly outdated, and even if they are not, people in the same job may perform the same tasks differently with equal results. Furthermore, the level of performance of the employee may be judged more on how well he or she gets along with others than how he or she adheres to the job description (Brethower, 1982).

Perhaps the point to be made from the criticisms of the typical job description is that it cannot be expected to accurately describe the standard by which the employee's performance will be measured. A job description can only be one of several inputs to the process of establishing a performance standard for the employee. In organizations where an employee is simply handed a job description and informed that it describes what he or she is expected to do, the above criticisms are certainly valid. However, if the other inputs to the appraisal system are used with the job description to establish what the desired performance is in a particular job, the job description may be as good a way as any of defining the job requirements for employees below the supervisor level.

A distinction should be made here between the job description and a job analysis. These two documents are usually intended for entirely different purposes. The job analysis is used to identify criteria that can be used to select a person with the right qualifications to fill a specific job. It is also used to establish a salary range for a job that will be consistent with the responsibilities and authority of the position and competitive with the salaries paid by other organizations. The job analysis made for these purposes is seldom effective in describing job requirements to employees (Schuster, 1985).

Expectations of supervisors and others. In addition to job requirements, role expectations are expressed by supervisors, peers in the same work group, and employees in other work groups whose roles are interrelated or complimentary. Supervisors express expectations by further allocating responsibilities, resources, authority, and facilities. Such allocations further define role expectations based on the abilities and needs of the employee.

Work group members and other employees also have expectations for the employee that are seldom described in a static job description. One of the "crucial" aspects of a job is "how" it is to be accomplished. To describe how a job is to be accomplished to an employee requires explaining what behaviors are expected in a wide range of contexts to include: (1) who the people are who have sensitive personalities and the kinds of relationships that have to be maintained, (2) the specific problems and barriers that must be met in the usual work schedule, (3) the historic blunders and frictions, (4) union relationships and how to deal with the union leaders, and (5) the specific integrative problems to be resolved. These and similar behaviors may be the true basis on which a person's performance will be judged (Levinson, 1979).

Efforts to explain the expectations of others is one of the purposes of team-building exercises. The focus of team building is to identify which behaviors by one member facilitates or impedes the effectiveness of other team members, and to teach employees to confront any difficulties among themselves openly and constructively. The intent is to enable people whose jobs require them to collaborate with each other to maximize their ability to facilitate each other's work and to minimize the interference of normal but dysfunctional events (Gellerman, 1972).

Supervisors need to become more sensitive to employee relationships and to realize that structuring these relationships can help them to influence employees without being heavy-handed or abrasive. Employees can do much for each other. They can respond to each other's needs, share their resources, and help each other develop efficient work methods and relationships (Tjosvold, 1983).

Employees' personalities, abilities, and needs. Because people are different, each employee brings to the appraisal process his or her unique personality, abilities, and set of needs (Maslow, 1954). Absolute congruence in what the organization expects of the employee and the unique characteristics of the employee are seldom, if ever, found in practice. For this reason, there are inevitable strains and conflicts of varying degrees between the individual and the organization. When there is conflict between personal needs and role expectations, and the employee chooses to fulfill personal needs, he or she is likely to do an unsatisfactory job of fulfilling role expectations. If the employee chooses to fulfill role expectations, he or she may become dissatisfied. In practice, the employee usually makes compromises that result in some amount of personal dissatisfaction and a performance that is below his or her maximum capability (Getzels & Guba, 1957).

The task of the supervisor is to integrate the individual into the job culture in a way that he or she may fulfill both organizational requirements and personal needs. The supervisor must focus on the unique characteristics of the individual that can be identified, and provide for them in the appraisal process. Providing for these characteristics means adjusting role expectations to avoid conflict, and providing the opportunity for the employee to satisfy his or her needs. The supervisor must also make the employee aware of adjustments that must be made in personal expectations in order to avoid role conflict. In any event, a degree of congruence must be achieved between role expectations and individual characteristics, and this must be accomplished by the appraisal process.

Although the expectations of employees for the job they are assigned may be different for each individual, it seems clear that employees hold some universal expectations of their supervisors. The following is a list of the most common of these expectations. The supervisor is usually expected to:

1. Assign challenging tasks that are consistent with abilities and training.
2. Clearly communicate the performance he or she expects and explain what contribution this will make to the organization.
3. Clearly establish the limits of authority and responsibility.
4. Permit freedom to perform the tasks assigned with minimum interference.
5. Listen to and consider new ideas and recommendations for change.
6. Provide for an environment which facilitates frank and open communication.
7. Maintain interpersonal relationships that permit the discussion of unresolved problems, soliciting and giving advice, receiving and giving constructive criticism, and exchanging unfavorable information without fear of destroying the relationship.
8. Be knowledgeable about his own job and be technically competent.
9. Maintain a calm professional approach in situations involving conflict.
10. Provide support when an employee is unfairly criticized.
11. Speak directly, and in private, about any displeasures he or she has with the work.
12. Provide appropriate rewards for accomplishments.
13. Assign or recommend employees for positions of greater responsibility when ability and initiative is demonstrated.
14. Provide assistance on tasks which prove to be beyond the capabilities or experience of an employee, or assign a job that is more consistent with current abilities and skills.
15. Know the decision-making process, and have the courage to share decisions at appropriate times.
16. Take the time to fully understand, evaluate, and critique the work of employees in a constructive way.

Formal methods of measuring performance. Most organizations use a combination of methods to measure the performance of employees annually or semiannually, and develop different rating forms for each family of jobs (Oberg, 1972). The methods used and the procedures for selecting and developing different rating forms are described in Chapter 8. These rating forms are inputs to the process of establishing the performance standards of employees because they identify what will be measured either annually or semiannually.

Since the same rating form is used to measure the performance of employees who work at similar jobs, what is measured may be described in more general terms than those used to describe the performance standard of a single employee. As a result, what is measured by the rating form is often interpreted differently by the employee and supervisor. These differences of interpretation are best resolved before the job commences rather than after the supervisor has rated the employee's performance.

The supervisor and employee should review the rating form that will be used, develop a mutual understanding of what it measures, identify the behaviors and outcomes that will be judged as evidence of good performance, and insure that there is a mutual understanding of what the performance rating will be used for. In many organizations an employee is never made aware of what is measured on these forms. As a result, the forms have no influence on the performance of the employee, and more often than not cause conflict and mistrust when the employee is informed of the rating given.

Knowledge of previous levels of performance. The last input to Process 1.1 is the knowledge the supervisor and employee have of the previous level of the employee's performance. If the performance met or exceeded the standard during previous cycles of the appraisal process, a new role may be devised that gives the employee greater responsibility and authority. If previous measures of performance have indicated areas where improvement is needed, this knowledge is used to establish a standard that can be achieved by the employee, or to plan specific actions that will assist the employee to achieve the standard expected by the organization. Such actions include providing additional training to improve the skills of the employee or coaching and counseling to provide incentives for improving performance.

SUPERVISOR DEVELOPS TENTATIVE STANDARD

In Process 1.2, Table 2, the supervisor develops a tentative performance standard for the employee based on his or her understanding of the inputs to the appraisal system. The objective of this process is to describe the role the employee is to play that accounts for not only the expectations of the organization but also the personality, abilities, wants, needs, and past performance of the employee. Developing the tentative standard also prepares the supervisor for discussions with the employee in which the final performance standard is established.

The tentative standard may be a general or detailed plan, depending on the level of participation desired or expected of the employee. If the employee is a manager or supervisor, the tentative standard may be made in outline form only. If the employee is below the supervisory level, the plan may be more detailed and include specific behaviors and outcomes. Tasks and responsibilities that are more important than others by virtue of their critical nature or the amount of time required to execute are identified and placed in order of priority (Boles & Davenport, 1975a).

When developing tentative performance standards, the supervisor should assign tasks to employees that capitalize on their most developed skills and that minimize the impact of their shortcomings. This may require changing some employees from one job to another, or revising all of the job descriptions within a work unit. The supervisor can also modify job descriptions based on the knowledge gained from the experiences of employees themselves to include better ways of accomplishing the same tasks. Since most of us like doing the things we do best, and prefer to do them our own way, such changes usually result in improved efficiency and less role conflict.

At this point in the process the supervisor may find that some employees have outgrown the jobs available within the work unit. In such cases the supervisor should recommend that these employees be transferred to other work units where their abilities and skills can be more fully utilized. Some writers have suggested that supervisors rarely make such recommendations because they do not want to lose good employees. Experience has shown, however, that such actions normally result in increased efficiency within all work units. Further, they demonstrate to employees that the supervisor recognizes and rewards good performance and that employees can influence their own futures by continuing to develop the skills needed by the organization.

When reassigning tasks the supervisor may also identify some employees whose skills need to be improved. If other employees in the work unit have demonstrated the needed skills, the supervisor may ask them to provide assistance to those who need it. If such actions cannot be taken within the work unit, action must be taken to obtain assistance from outside of the work unit. If neither of these two courses of action can be taken, it is necessary for the supervisor to request that personnel be transferred into and out of the work unit to satisfy the skill requirements. Supervisors who have the ability to accomplish the tasks assigned without asking for outside help are usually highly valued by their superiors. There are times, however, when even the most accomplished supervisor needs assistance.

EMPLOYEE DEVELOPS TENTATIVE STANDARD

In Process 1.3, Table 2, the employee develops his or her own tentative performance standard. The objective of this process is for the employee to generate a description of how he or she sees the role assigned. This can be a simple thought process that clarifies his or her role expectations or it can be a detailed formal plan for achieving the goals of the organization within his or her area of responsibility. The type of plan the employee is expected to develop depends on the job level and past experience, competence, and maturity of the employee. Other factors may include the extent to which the employee has been informed of the overall requirements of the organization, and the amount of change expected in his or her assigned tasks (Boles & Davenport, 1975a). In any case, the employee should participate in this process to the extent that he or she is prepared to discuss the final performance standard with the supervisor.

The employee should be prepared to recommend changes in procedures and practices, based on his or her experience, that will improve effectiveness in the job and keep role conflict to a minimum. Many organizations have initiated programs such as Quality Circles to generate such recommendations from selected groups of employees. Most often, however, these programs have failed to provide the opportunity for all employees to make contributions. One innovative method of providing the opportunity for effective information sharing uses computer records of job descriptions. When needed, a computer-generated job description is given to the employee to review and make any necessary additions or deletions to update the information. The corrected copy is then given to his or her immediate supervisor as an input to the process of establishing the employee's performance standard. Once the final performance standard is established, the job description is updated and entered into the computer data file.

ESTABLISH FINAL PERFORMANCE STANDARD

The final performance standard to which the employee's performance will be compared during the appraisal period is established in Process 1.4, Table 2. The supervisor and employee discuss the two tentative performance standards they have developed and reconcile any differences between them.

This process may be carried out in a number of different ways depending on the level of the job and the personalities involved. More participation should be expected from employees who are managers or supervisors and from employees at lower levels who work independently. The process might consist of a briefing where the employee explains his or her plan of action and requests the concurrence of the supervisor. On the other hand, it might consist of a negotiation between the supervisor and the employee where both present their version of the performance standard, and the differences are resolved through discussion. In either case, the supervisor will normally make the final decision. If the employee has performed the job before, and there is no change in inputs, the supervisor may simply inform the employee what the performance standard will be (Brethower, 1982).

Regardless of the form it takes, the supervisor should make sure that the employee has the necessary information about the organization, the department goals the employee is expected to support, any assignments that he or she has decided that the employee must undertake, and the probable ground rules for accomplishing the assignment. The supervisor and the employee should review the major steps for accomplishing the assigned tasks, including: timing, priorities, and resources. The employee should also be given the opportunity to suggest changes and to ask questions about those parts of the standard that are not clearly understood (Kellogg, 1965d).

When documented, the performance standard becomes the broad plan for the employee's work. It permits the employee to see what he or she will be doing and the results that this work is expected to achieve. It also permits the employee to make judgments about the adequacy of his or her work, obtain feedback from the technical side of the work, and to make adjustments in performance where necessary. The standard also provides a checklist of the things the supervisor must observe and measure during the appraisal period.

The performance standard may be expressed in terms of quality and quantity of work, work behaviors, goals or objectives, and a combination of these terms.

Regardless of the terms used, it is basically a goal or target to shoot for. Communicating these goals to achieve understanding can be facilitated or impeded by a number of things.

Things that facilitate good communication of goals include: (1) stating them in measurable terms; (2) stating short-term goals or subgoals to be used as benchmarks in measuring progress; (3) stating how measurements of progress, or lack of it, will be used by management; and (4) setting the goals in direct two-way communication with those whose performance is affected. The pitfalls to be avoided in setting goals include: (1) setting conflicting goals; (2) maximizing the efficiency of one employee, thereby forcing inefficiency of another; (3) ignoring realistic constraints; (4) setting goals in conflict with larger goals; (5) failing to set subgoals so the performer can see how day-to-day performance relates to them; (6) failing to set priorities; and (7) setting goals too high or too low (Brethower, 1982).

The objectives of Process 1.4, Table 2, are: (1) to establish a standard to which the employee's performance will be compared during the appraisal period, (2) to achieve congruence, in so far as possible, between what the organization expects of the employee and what the employee expects of his or her job, and (3) to develop a mutual understanding between the supervisor and the employee as to what the performance standard is.

Achieving congruence and mutual understanding by this process alone is very difficult. A lack of congruence can result from a lack of understanding of the employee's abilities and needs on the part of the supervisor. It can also be the result of a lack of opportunity within the work unit to take full advantage of the employee's skills or unrealistic expectations on the part of the employee. Therefore, necessary adjustments in the standard may be best identified during the time that the work is actually being performed. If the supervisor judges that the expectations of the employee are unrealistic, he or she should encourage the employee to make a more realistic evaluation of the facts and to develop a plan for achieving his or her expectations in the future.

Other possible objectives for this process are suggested by the literature on performance appraisal in the context of the value of participation of the employee. The three objectives that are most often suggested are: (1) to obtain "agreement" with the performance standard, (2) to obtain "acceptance" of the performance standard, and (3) to "motivate" the employee. Some research has indicated there is a relationship between the participation of the employee in goal setting and goal acceptance. Other studies have indicated that goals assigned by the supervisor may be more readily accepted by some employees (Dossett, Latham, & Mitchell, 1979). The implications are that supervisors need to recognize the differences in individuals, and deal with each in a way that is most likely to maximize his or her performance.

The problem with objectives such as "acceptance," "agreement," and "motivation" is that they purport to describe a condition that is internal to the employee and which is difficult to define, let alone communicate. Further, the employee must decide whether to communicate these conditions or not, and if he or she chooses not to, they are difficult for the supervisor to observe and measure. Participation in establishing the performance standard may make some contribution to achieving these objectives, but whether it does or does not depends more on the individual involved than the process.

Although there may be some question about the objectives of employee participation, there is general agreement that the employee should participate. Whoever has the final responsibility for setting the standard should do so in direct communication with the person whose performance is to be judged. The employee's contribution may involve providing information about capabilities and constraints, participating in a discussion where the manager makes the final decision, or participating in a democratic process that culminates in a vote. But whatever form it takes, the employee should be involved in setting the standard. Anything else would require that managers and supervisors set performance standards without making use of information that employees have that is directly relevant and readily available (Brethower, 1982).

CONSEQUENCES OF FAILURE

In addition to being able to recognize when a system is not working, we must be able to identify the causes and assess the consequences of failure. The causes must be known if effective changes are to be made. We need to know the consequences of failure to make decisions about initiating changes. Changes that are not likely to make a noticeable difference may not be worth the time and effort.

Identifying the causes and assessing the consequences of failure are difficult tasks when the system is as complex as performance appraisal. However, when the system is broken down into its component parts, these tasks become much easier. For example, if the policies and procedures of an organization are not included as inputs and discussed by the supervisor and employee in the first step of the appraisal process, there are likely to be differences of opinion about what they are and what they do and do not mean.

The consequences of failure can be identified for each input, process, and objective by asking "what if" type questions. The answers to these questions can be used to identify parts that are failing, and to assess the risks resulting from failure. The symptoms or risks were identified for Subsystem 1.0, Table 2, by asking these questions. They are listed below under the process in which the failure is likely to occur.

Process 1.1

What if supervisors and employees do not review all of the inputs to the performance appraisal system?

- There may be differences of opinion about the philosophy, policies, procedures, and rules of the organization.
- Supervisors and employees may interpret job requirements differently.
- Supervisors may not explain the expectations that others have for the person assigned a specific job.
- Supervisors and employees may not know or understand what will be measured by the annual or semiannual performance ratings.
- Supervisors may not identify the abilities, wants, and needs of employees.
- Supervisors and employees may not identify and plan actions that are needed to improve performance.

Process 1.2

What if supervisors do not use the information obtained in Process 1.1 to develop a tentative performance standard for the employee?

- Supervisors may not accurately identify or plan what is expected of employees.
- Supervisors may fail to make adjustments in job descriptions that improve efficiency and help avoid role conflict for employees.
- Supervisors may not be prepared to effectively communicate their expectations to employees.

Process 1.3

What if employees do not use the information obtained in Process 1.1 and develop their own tentative performance standards?

- Employees may not be prepared to participate in establishing the final performance standard and they may not fully understand what is expected of them when the standard is established.
- Employees may not provide information to their supervisors that would improve performance and efficiency.
- The situations that are likely to cause role conflict and low performance may not be identified.

Process 1.4

What if supervisors and employees do not reconcile the differences in their perceptions of what the performance standards are?

- A valid standard is not likely to be established on which to base appraisals of performance.
- There may be a lack of mutual understanding about what is being appraised.

- They may disagree about what should be an adequate performance.
- Conflict may occur during work until differences are resolved.
- Employees may not be able to collect the right information to judge and correct their own performances.
- Employees may not have, understand, or use their authority and initiative to improve job procedures.
- The strengths of employees may not be fully utilized nor weaknesses minimized.
- Employees may experience role conflict, limiting their effectiveness and causing dissatisfaction.
- A valid verifiable basis for the appraisal process may not be established.

SUMMARY

In the first subsystem of appraisal the supervisor and the employee establish the standard to which the employee's performance will be compared during the appraisal period. An effort is made to develop a mutual understanding of how the inputs to the appraisal system should be interpreted and the standard by which the employee's performance will be judged. Both the supervisor and the employee develop a tentative standard and resolve any differences through discussion. They then attempt to develop a standard that will satisfy the expectations of the organization and, at the same time, those of the employee. To the extent possible, congruence of role expectations and employee expectations is sought which serves to avoid role conflict.

The performance standard can be documented through a number of different formats but it must, in any case, identify the tasks to be carried out by the employee, and express them in terms of results (outcomes) and activities (behaviors) that are necessary to achieve these results. In addition, the standard should assign a priority for each task.

REFERENCES

Boles, H. W., & Davenport, J. A. (1975a). Role expectations. In *Introduction to educational leadership*. New York: Harper and Row, pp. 21–43.

Boles, H. W., & Davenport, J. A. (1975b). Leaders and expectations. In *Introduction to educational leadership*. New York: Harper and Row, pp. 44–63.

Brethower, D. M. (1982). The total performance system. In R. M. O'Brien, A. M. Dickinson, & M. P. Roscow (Eds.), *Industrial behavior modification: A management handbook*. New York: Pergamon Press, pp. 350–369.

Cocheu, T. (1986). Performance appraisal: A case in point. *Personnel Journal, 65*(September): 48–55.

Davidson, J. P. (1981). Communicating company objectives. *Personnel Journal, 60*(April): 479–493.

Delamontagne, R. P. & Weitzul, J. B. (1980). Performance alignment: The fine art of the perfect fit. *Personnel Journal, 59*(February): 115–117.

Dipboye, R. L., & de Pontbriand, R. (1981). Correlates of employee reactions to performance appraisals and appraisal systems. *Journal of Applied Psychology, 66*(2): 248–251.

Dossett, D. L., Latham, G. P., & Mitchell, T. R. (1979). Effects of assigned versus participatively set goals, knowledge of results, and individual differences on employee behavior when goal difficulty is held constant. *Journal of Applied Psychology, 64*(3): 291–298.

Gellerman, S. W. (1972). Motivation and performance. In J. J. Famularo (Ed.), *Handbook of modern personnel administration*. New York: McGraw-Hill, pp. 2–1 to 2–7.

Getzels, J. W., & Guba, E. G. (1957). Social behavior and the administrative process. *School Review, 65*(4): 423–441.

Herzberg, F. (1968). One more time: How do you motivate employees? *Harvard Business Review, 46*(1): 53–62.

Herzberg, F., Mausner, B., & Snyderman, B. (1959). *The Motivation to work*. New York: John Wiley & Sons.

Iwanicki, E. F. (1981). Contract plans: A professional growth-oriented approach to evaluating teacher performance. In J. Millman (Ed.), *Handbook of teacher evaluation*. Beverly Hills, CA: Sage, pp. 203–228.

Kaye, B. L., & Krantz, S. (1982). Preparing employees: The missing link in performance appraisal training. *Personnel, 59*(3): 23–29.

Kellogg, M. S. (1965d). Work planning and progress review. In *What to do about performance appraisal*. New York: American Management Association, pp. 68–82.

Latham, G. P., & Yukl, G. A. (1975). A review of research on the application of goal setting in organizations. *Academy of Management Journal, 18*(12): 824–845.

Levinson, H. (1979). Appraisal of what performance? In Harvard Business Review (Eds.), *Harvard Business Review on Human Relations*. New York: Harper and Row, pp. 280–292.

Lopez, F. M. (1968a). Significance of the setting. In *Evaluating employee performance*. Chicago: Public Personnel Association, pp. 43–55.

Lopez, F. M. (1968d). Measuring human performance. In *Evaluating employee performance*. Chicago: Public Personnel Association, pp. 163–286.

Maslow, A. H. (1954). *Motivation and personality*. New York: Harper and Row.

Oberg, W. (1972). Make performance appraisal relevant. *Harvard Business Review, 50*(1): 61–76.

Schoderbek, P. P., & Reif, W. E. (1969). Introduction. In *Job enlargement: Key to improving performance*. Ann Arbor: University of Michigan, Bureau of Industrial Relations, pp. 7–25.

Schuster, J. R. (1985). How to control job evaluation inflation. *Personnel Administrator, 30*(6): 167–173.

Stedry, A. C., & Kay, E. (1966). The effects of goal difficulty on performance: A field experiment. *Behavioral Science, 11*: 459–470.

Tjosvold, D. (1983). Managing peer relationships among subordinates. *Personnel, 60*(6): 13–22.

Tosi, H. L., Rizzo, J. R., & Carroll, S. J. (1970). Setting goals in management by objective. *California Management Review, 12*(4): 70–78.

White, S. E., & Mitchell, T. R. (1979). Job enrichment versus social cues: A comparison and competitive test. *Journal of Applied Psychology, 64*(1): 1–9.

CHAPTER 5

Helping Employees Perform Up to Standard

In the second step of the typical performance appraisal strategy, employees perform the tasks assigned. During this period it is the responsibility of supervisors to assist employees to perform up to standard. The steps that are necessary for supervisors to carry out this responsibility are the components of Subsystem 2.0, Table 1, of appraisal. In general terms these steps include observing and appraising performance, providing feedback, coaching, removing blocks to good performance, and providing incentives to improve poor performance.

Much of the criticism of performance appraisal systems stem from the conclusion that supervisors do not, or cannot, accomplish these tasks during the work period. The reasons frequently given are: insufficient time, too much paperwork, too many employees to supervise, too many other duties, and too many problems to solve that require immediate attention. If, however, the tasks are not performed, poor performance is not likely to improve, inefficiency will continue, and it is unlikely that the system will produce valid measures of performance.

A fact that is not always recognized is that supervisors provide some type of feedback to employees all of the time, whether intended or not. Further, many of the immediate problems that consume the supervisor's time are themselves caused by providing the wrong kinds of feedback. If the supervisor is seldom seen in the work area, he or she may be telling employees that the level of their performance is not important enough to be concerned about. By passing through the work area each day, and making friendly remarks and small talk, the supervisor may be telling employees that he or she is satisfied with their level of performance, even if it is below standard. Employees may also get the impression that the supervisor does not know enough about their work to judge their level of performance or to recognize and provide assistance in situations where it is needed. With this type of dysfunctional feedback, employees are usually very surprised and angry when they receive anything less than a high rating on their annual or semiannual review. Supervisors who do not find time to observe performance and provide assistance and feedback during the work period must choose between giving all employees high ratings or making judgments of lesser levels of performance based on insufficient information and casual observation. Usually ratings are inflated to avoid making unfair judgments or to avoid conflict with employees.

There are a number of steps that must be taken by the supervisor to make fair and accurate judgments of the performance of employees, to assist them to perform up to standard, and to determine what type of feedback should be given. These steps or processes and their objectives are shown in Table 3.

COACHING AND COLLECTING INFORMATION ON PERFORMANCE

In Process 2.1, Table 3, the supervisor coaches the employee and both collect information on the employee's performance. The objectives of this process are to insure that the performance standard is understood, to obtain measures of the employee's performance, and to assist the employee.

The coaching relationship should be a two-way communication process. The supervisor makes sure that there is no misunderstanding of the assigned tasks and the results the employee is expected to achieve. The supervisor shares whatever knowledge, skill, or experience he or she has that will contribute to the successful accomplishment of the tasks and reinforces the employee's behaviors that have led to success. The employee fulfills his or her part by applying full competence to the task, identifying and communicating actions that he or she feels can improve efficiency, seeking help when needed, and keeping the supervisor informed of his or her progress (Kellogg, 1965a).

The coaching relationship assumes that, until proven otherwise, the employee wants to do a good job. If the employee does not do a good job, it is assumed that he or she does not know how to accomplish the assigned tasks. The actions of the supervisor are directed to teaching the employee to perform up to standard.

The importance of the performance standard in collecting information about the level of performance of the employee is illustrated by the cognitive processes that are carried out. These processes include: (1) recognizing and collecting relevant information, (2) organizing and storing the information for later use, (3) integrating new information as it is gathered, and (4) recalling and summarizing the information in a way that will permit a comparison with the standard. Since impressions and evaluations are formed as behavior is observed sequentially, final judgments may be based as much on memory as on current observation. To the degree that the behavior of the employee is consistent with expectations, it is noted and stored automatically. It may be that only when behavior departs from expectations, or when the task is somehow changed, that conscious attention and recognition processes are engaged. The performance standard describes the expectations that guide the cognitive processes of both the supervisor and the employee. It is crucial, however, that the supervisor make

Table 3
Subsystem 2.0: Observe and Coach Employee

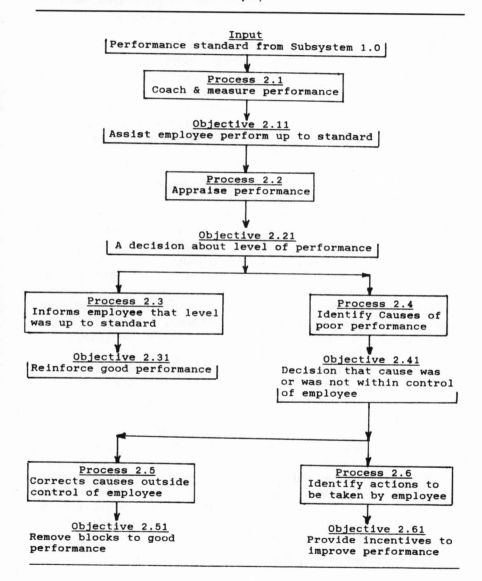

Input
Performance standard from Subsystem 1.0

Process 2.1
Coach & measure performance

Objective 2.11
Assist employee perform up to standard

Process 2.2
Appraise performance

Objective 2.21
A decision about level of performance

Process 2.3
Informs employee that level was up to standard

Process 2.4
Identify Causes of poor performance

Objective 2.31
Reinforce good performance

Objective 2.41
Decision that cause was or was not within control of employee

Process 2.5
Corrects causes outside control of employee

Process 2.6
Identify actions to be taken by employee

Objective 2.51
Remove blocks to good performance

Objective 2.61
Provide incentives to improve performance

a conscious effort to recognize when the employee is performing up to expectations. Only in this way can he or she be able to provide feedback to reinforce good performance (Feldman, 1981).

Research in the field of behavioral science has provided guidance in regard to who should measure performance, and how and when performance should be measured. Ideally, performance should be measured continuously. However, some behaviors do not lend themselves to continuous measurement and organizational constraints may make it impossible. Supervisors cannot constantly record the performance of several employees and such recording would disrupt the unit's work. But data can be collected by the employee, the supervisor, and other employees. Having the employee keep track of his or her own performance has the advantage of providing immediate feedback. The disadvantage is that the employee may measure only those things that he or she sees that are favorable. However, the supervisor can encourage and reinforce accurate and reliable self-recording (Dickinson & O'Brien, 1982).

Other employees in the work group and other work groups will measure or form perceptions of the employee's performance whether or not they are required to do so. These measurements and perceptions may be difficult for the supervisor to obtain, but they have great importance for the employee. Often such judgments are based on faulty information or personal likes or dislikes. Nevertheless, they may identify problem areas that need to be addressed. Solving these problems entails resolving misunderstandings, improving communication, changing the behavior of the employee, or simply allowing the employee to work the problem out for him or herself. The supervisor should not be too quick to confront the employee or to defend the employee against all accusations. He or she must defend employees when they are right, but even a strong defense may not solve the problem. The solution involves resolving disagreements, correcting misinformation, and coaching the employee.

Organizations often make the mistake of relying only on output measures when judging performance that may reflect circumstances outside the control of the employee. For example, the quality and quantity of output of an assembly line worker often depends on the speed of the assembly line belt, other employees on the line, and the quality of parts coming to the employee. Outcome measures may fail to provide the employee with sufficient and timely feedback, and they fail to specify the behaviors that must occur to obtain the desired results. Even those situations when output adequately reflects performance, the supervisor may still not know what should be reinforced or changed. Although outcomes are useful in identifying performance deficiencies, they must be supplemented with measures of behavior (Dickinson & O'Brien, 1982).

COMPARING PERFORMANCE MEASURES WITH STANDARD

In Process 2.2, Table 3, the supervisor decides if the employee's performance is or is not up to standard by comparing the measures with the performance standard. Several such appraisals may be made during the period between annual or semiannual performance reviews. The period covered by each of these comparisons may vary depending on a number of circumstances. These include: (1) the need to provide feedback to the employee; (2) how serious a failure would be for the organization and the employee, (3) the time required to produce a measurable result; (4) deadlines, target dates, and production schedules; (5) events generated by other parts of the organization, and (6) other factors that may be unique to the job, the employee, or the organization.

If the performance standard of the employee describes specific behaviors and outcomes it may be possible for the supervisor to make a completely objective decision about the level of performance of the employee. However, if the performance standard is described in general terms the decision may not be that simple. For example, a performance standard may include behaviors such as, "maintain satisfactory working relationships with other members of the work group," or "provide on-the-job training as necessary to improve and maintain the skills of the work group." Deciding if these general behaviors and outcomes were carried out and their objectives achieved is likely to require a subjective judgement based on observations that cannot be quantified. It is also necessary to evaluate and verify the accuracy of information on which the decision must be based by further investigation and discussion with the employee.

The environment of the work place is constantly changed by a multitude of variables. Some of these variables can be identified and the changes anticipated, but others may affect performance in ways that are unpredictable. It is necessary, therefore, to review and revise the performance standard when experience indicates that it is set too high or too low.

If the supervisor judges the performance of the employee to be up to standard, he or she provides feedback in Process 2.3, Table 3. If the supervisor judges that there is a performance discrepancy, he or she decides if it is important enough to warrant corrective action. If worthwhile results can be obtained through some action, the supervisor must go further to determine the cause of the discrepancy in Process 2.4, Table 3.

REINFORCING GOOD PERFORMANCE

In Process 2.3, the supervisor informs the employee that his or her performance is up to standard and explains the measures on which this judgment was made. The objectives of this process are to reinforce good performance and to keep the employee informed of the factors considered in the appraisal.

If good performance is to be maintained, it must be reinforced on a continuing basis. A system which gives the supervisor and the employee routine information on the quality and quantity of the performance helps to provide timely feedback. With this type of interactive system, occasional supervisor recognition may be all that is required. A reasonably good rule of thumb is that a supervisor should make a point of reinforcing good performance, in one way or another, at least once a week. When an employee starts a new job, reinforcement should be frequent, but gradually the supervisor contacts can be reduced to a steady, less frequent schedule (Brethower, 1982).

Methods of providing feedback include: (1) showing the employee the results of a sampling of his or her performance; (2) personal conferences and reviews; (3) day-to-day comments, such as, "That's good work"; (4) encouraging self-evaluation; (5) posting performance statistics; (6) using automatic recording devices to measure output; (7) quality control programs; and (8) graphic displays of performance measures.

Feedback is ordinarily most effective when given as soon as possible after the work is completed. However, when deciding when to give feedback these questions should be asked: "Can it be used to guide performance?" and "Is there a time when these comments would be more useful?" (Brethower, 1982).

IDENTIFYING CAUSES OF POOR PERFORMANCE

If the supervisor judges the performance of the employee to be below standard, he or she cannot assume that it was the fault of the employee. In Process 2.4, Table 3, the supervisor and the employee work together to identify the cause and to determine if it was within or outside the control of the employee. If it is determined that the cause was outside the control of the employee, it is the supervisor's responsibility to remove the cause of the dysfunction. If the cause was within the control of the employee, it is usually considered a problem of motivation which may require some type of incentive to correct the problem.

Causes Outside the Control of the Employee

Inadequate performance can be caused by circumstances and conditions beyond the control of the employee. These may include: (1) poor policies and procedures, (2) inadequate job design, (3) faulty measures of performance, (4) ineffective communication of the performance standard, (5) inadequate tools and materials, (6) lack of knowledge or skills, and (7) ineffective training (Mager & Pipe, 1970).

Examples of performance deficiencies that are outside the control of the employee can be found in nearly all organizations. One that comes to mind involves the parts clerks of a department of a large organization. The parts section of the department never seemed to be able to obtain the parts required when needed. Nevertheless, the records indicated that the funds allocated to the departments for parts were usually all committed or spent by the middle of the fiscal year. This problem had existed for two or three years even though supervisors and clerks had been replaced and a great deal of time and effort was spent on the training of personnel.

When a new department manager arrived he decided to investigate the problem further. An examination of the records indicated that employees had been following established policies and procedures, but there was a large number of unfilled requisitions for parts in the files. Further investigation revealed that the problem was at the computer center of the organization.

If the parts were not on hand in the organization supply when requisitioned by a department, the computer initiated a purchase order, and gave the department a due out. When the parts were received by the organization supply the computer identified the department to receive them based on a preestablished priority. Departments with low priorities received their parts last, provided sufficient parts were received by the organization. Because of a faulty program, the computer deleted the records of unfilled requisitions of departments with low priorities when the parts they had requested were issued to other departments with higher priorities. Because the parts were charged to the accounts of departments when the requisitions were submitted, the records indicated that low priority departments usually ran out of funds, and accumulated large numbers of unfilled requisitions in their files.

To correct the problem, the computer program was changed so that unfilled requisitions were not cancelled, and departments were not charged for parts until they were actually received from the organizational supply. As a result of these changes, parts were received, and the departments remained within budget.

For several years the performance of supervisors and parts clerks had been judged deficient because of faulty procedures beyond their control. The cost in terms of personnel and resources was much greater than that required to identify and correct the true cause of the problem.

Causes Within the Control of the Employee

Some of the causes of unsatisfactory performance that may be within the control of the employee include: poor relationships with other members of the work group or other work groups; dissatisfaction with the supervisor, policies, or procedures; lack of acceptance of the performance standard; and problems at home. Motivational problems may also be due to a lack of social or monetary incentives (Mager & Pipe, 1970).

REMOVING BLOCKS TO GOOD PERFORMANCE

If the supervisor and employee determine that a performance discrepancy is due to causes outside the control of the employee, action is taken by the supervisor in Process 2.5, Table 3, to correct the problem. The supervisor also makes sure that the employee knows the cause of the performance discrepancy and the actions that he or she has taken to correct the problem. The objectives are to remove blocks to good performance and to maintain the confidence of the employee in the appraisal system.

Some methods of removing blocks to a good performance are: (1) improving tools, materials, or the work environment; (2) providing training to develop the necessary skill; (3) revising the performance standard; (4) improving the way performance is measured; or (5) communicating the performance standard more clearly to the employee.

PROVIDING FEEDBACK TO IMPROVE MOTIVATION

If the supervisor and employee determine that a performance discrepancy is within the control of the employee, action is taken in Process 2.6, Table 3, to improve motivation. The objective is to provide incentives and a plan for improving the employee's performance. Motivational theorists occasionally disagree about how to define "incentives," and about what kinds of incentives should be used. But, all agree that incentives are necessary.

Research suggests that at least 90 percent of the so-called motivational problems can be solved by using one of five possible reinforcers. They are: (1) regular feedback on job performance, (2) regular feedback on performance improvement, (3) regular feedback on progress toward goals, (4) positive supervisor comments on good performance, and (5) positive supervisor comments on performance improvement (Brethower, 1982).

CONSEQUENCES OF FAILURE

The consequences of failure resulting from discrepancies in the design or operation of Subsystem 2.0 are listed below. These symptoms or risks were identified by asking the questions: "What if this input is not used?"; "What if this process is not carried out?"; and "What if this objective is not achieved?"

Process 2.1

What if supervisors do not coach employees, and both supervisors and employees do not collect information on activities and outputs?

- Differences in perceptions of performance standards may not be identified or reconciled.
- Job related measures of performance may not be obtained or recorded.
- Coaching to assist employees in succeeding will not be given when needed.
- Employees may not collect or recognize the information necessary to correct their own performance.
- Poor performances are not likely to be improved nor good performances recognized or rewarded.
- Formal measures of performance may be challenged if they cannot be supported with job related measures, the performance standards are not understood, or there is no coaching during the appraisal period.

Process 2.2

What if supervisors do not appraise observed performance by comparing it to performance standards?

- Good, poor, and marginal performances may not be recognized or detected until the end of the appraisal period when performance ratings are prepared.

Process 2.3

What if supervisors do not inform employees when their performance is up to standard and explain the measures on which these judgments were based?

- The performance of good employees may decline without reinforcement.
- Employees may not be aware of the activities and achievements that were measured and how they were judged by supervisors.
- Supervisors may concentrate on employees who perform poorly.
- Good performers may feel that good performance goes unrecognized.

Process 2.4

What if supervisors and employees do not work together to identify the causes of poor performance?

- Good workers may be judged poor performers when the causes are beyond their control.
- The real causes of poor performance may go undetected and poor performance may be allowed to continue.
- Unless employees participate, the real causes may not be identified and judgments of fault may not be accepted or performance improved.

Process 2.5

What if supervisors do not correct the causes of poor performance that are outside the control of employees?

- Poor performance and inefficiency will continue.
- Supervisors may lose the faith, trust, and respect of their employees.
- Good employees may be lost because of lack of job satisfaction.

Process 2.6

What if supervisors do not inform employees when poor performance is judged to be within their control and inform them of the actions they should take to improve their performance?

- Poor performance will continue.

- Employees may be transferred to other jobs and continue low performance.

- Conflict may be generated by workers who do not do their jobs when no action is taken by supervisors.

- The organization will be vulnerable to court actions if ineffective employees are terminated and no assistance has been given to improve their performance.

SUMMARY

Subsystem 2.0 of the appraisal system can be summarized as a series of steps designed to identify and provide the feedback needed to perform up to standard. These steps include: coaching and measuring the performance of employees, appraising performance by comparing it to performance standards, identifying the causes of poor performance, removing blocks to good performance, providing feedback to reinforce good performance, and providing incentives for improving poor performance.

This subsystem is a continuous cycle that can be undertaken several times during the period covered by annual or semiannual performance ratings. The actions of the supervisor are directed to assisting the employee to perform up to standard. The annual or semiannual performance rating prepared in the next step of appraisal is actually a summary of the appraisals made when carrying out the processes of this subsystem. It may not be appropriate to include in a performance summary any shortcomings of the employee that have not been previously discussed with the employee.

REFERENCES

Brethower, D. M. (1982). The total performance system. In R. M. O'Brien, A. M. Dickinson, & M. P. Roscow (Eds.), *Industrial behavior modification: A management handbook*. New York: Pergamon Press, pp. 350–369.

Dickinson, A. M., & O'Brien, R. M. (1982). Performance measurement and evaluation. In R. M. O'Brien, A. M. Dickinson, & M. P. Roscow (Eds.), *Industrial behavior modification: A management handbook*. New York: Pergamon Press, pp. 51–64.

Feldman, J. M. (1981). Beyond attribution theory: Cognitive processes in performance appraisal. *Journal of Applied Psychology, 66*(2): 127–148.

Ilgen, D. R., Fisher, C. D., & Taylor, M. S. (1979). Consequences of individual feedback on behavior in organizations. *Journal of Applied Psychology, 64*(4): 349–371.

Jackson, S. E., & Zedeck, S. (1982). Explaining performance variability: Conditions of goal setting, task characteristics, and evaluation contexts. *Journal of Applied Psychology, 67*(6): 759–768.

Kellogg, M. S. (1965a). The coaching appraisal. In *What to do about performance appraisal*. New York: American Management Association, pp. 31–41.

Kellogg, M. S. (1965b). Before discussing the coaching appraisal. In *What to do about performance appraisal*. New York: American Management Association, pp. 43–52.

Kellogg, M. S. (1965c). Applying the coaching appraisal. In *What to do about performance appraisal*. New York: American Management Association, pp. 53–67.

Kellogg, M. S. (1965e). What about personality? In *What to do about performance appraisal*. New York: American Management Association, pp. 83–93.

Lawler, E. E., III, & Porter, L. W. (1967). The effect of performance on job satisfaction. *Industrial Relations, 10*(7): 20–28.

Mager, R. F., & Pipe, P. (1970). *Analyzing performance problems or "you really oughta wanna."* Belmont, CA: Fearon Publishers.

Matejka, J. K., Ashworth, D. N., & Dodd-McCue, D. (1986). Managing difficult employees: Challenge or curse? *Personnel, 63*(7): 43–46.

McFarland, R. A. (1971). Understanding fatigue in modern life. *Ergonomics, 14*(1): 1–10.

Mischkind, L. A. (1986). Is employee morale hidden behind statistics? *Personnel Journal, 65*(February): 74–79.

Morano, R. A. (1974). A new concept in personnel development and employee relations. *Personnel Journal, 53*(August): 606–611.

Sergiovanni, T. J., & Starratt, R. J. (1979). *Supervision: Human perspective* (2nd ed.). New York: McGraw-Hill, pp. 98–130.

Shore, L. M., & Bloom, A. J. (1986). Developing employees through coaching and career management. *Personnel, 63*(8): 34–41.

Snell, S. A., & Wexley, K. N. (1985). Poor performance diagnosis: Identifying the cause of poor performance. *Personnel Administration, 30*(4): 117–127.

CHAPTER 6

Completing Performance Summaries

The third step of the typical appraisal strategy, Table 1, is to complete a formal summary of the performance of employees to cover a specific period of time. The supervisor is provided with a standard form to complete that has been designed to measure the performance of the employee. The primary objective of this subsystem is to produce a measure of performance with minimum administrative and human error. A number of procedures are included in this subsystem to detect and correct error before it becomes a part of the permanent record and before it influences the future of employees in the organization. These procedures include the participation of the employee, the second-level supervisor, and a personnel specialist. They also include the participation of higher levels of supervision and a board of review when performance ratings are challenged by employees.

The inputs, processes, and objectives of Subsystem 3.0 are shown in Table 4. The inputs are the policies and procedures of the organization, the methods and rating forms used, the informal appraisals made during the period covered by the summary, and the feedback given the employee during the period.

POLICIES AND PROCEDURES

Policies and procedures pertaining to the formal summary of performance usually establish the frequency and timing of their preparation and assign responsibilities for their preparation and review. Summaries are normally prepared for managers and supervisors annually, and semiannually for employees below the supervisor level. Summaries may be prepared for all members of a work group at the same time, or one member at a time based on some anniversary such as the date of employment (Lopez, 1968d).

Some personnel managers advocate spreading performance summaries out over a period of time by using an anniversary date of each employee. In theory, if the supervisor can take more time to complete the forms there will be less opportunity for error. There are, however, reasons to question this practice. If

Table 4
Subsystem 3.0: Complete Formal Summary of Performance

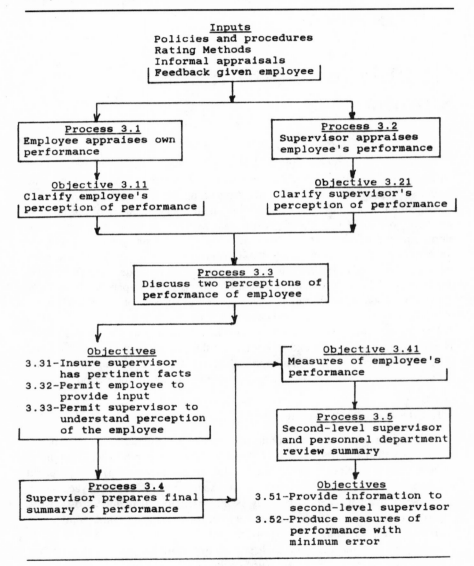

Inputs
Policies and procedures
Rating Methods
Informal appraisals
Feedback given employee

Process 3.1
Employee appraises own
performance

Process 3.2
Supervisor appraises
employee's performance

Objective 3.11
Clarify employee's
perception of performance

Objective 3.21
Clarify supervisor's
perception of performance

Process 3.3
Discuss two perceptions of
performance of employee

Objectives
3.31-Insure supervisor
has pertinent facts
3.32-Permit employee to
provide input
3.33-Permit supervisor to
understand perception
of the employee

Objective 3.41
Measures of employee's
performance

Process 3.5
Second-level supervisor
and personnel department
review summary

Process 3.4
Supervisor prepares final
summary of performance

Objectives
3.51-Provide information to
second-level supervisor
3.52-Produce measures of
performance with
minimum error

they are prepared on anniversary dates that are different for each employee, they will cover different periods of time for the members of a work group. Therefore, they may not provide a valid basis for comparing performance ratings of employees in the work group. There will always be members of the work group that have not received a recent rating when personnel decisions are made.

The theory that less error will be made when summaries are spread out is also questionable. In fact, there is reason to believe that they will contain more error. If performance ratings are completed at different times for members of a work group, supervisors are likely to have difficulty being consistent. They may have no way of knowing that the ratings reflect the order-of-merit of the members of the work group, or if the best performers receive the highest ratings and the poorest performers the lowest ratings. If ratings do not differentiate between the levels of performance of employees they are not very useful when making management decisions.

It seems advisable to complete performance summaries for all employees who are rated using the same form at the same time (Fishback, 1972). The supervisor can then use an order-of-merit to insure that the ratings are consistent. The ratings may still contain human error, but they should differentiate between the levels of performance within the work group. Human error is much easier to detect and correct when all ratings are completed at the same time. Further, the date of completing the ratings can be established to provide up-to-date information when management decisions are to be made. For example, if decisions are made about merit pay, training, and career development at a specific time of the year for budgeting purposes, a date can be established to insure that up-to-date ratings are available at that time. Such procedures should save time for supervisors in the long run because they would simplify, and perhaps eliminate, some procedures for recommending employees for personnel actions. Procedures for identifying human error are described in Chapter 10.

EMPLOYEE PROVIDES INFORMATION

In Process 3.1, Table 4, the employee provides information to the supervisor about his or her perception of the level of performance and may prepare a summary of his or her own performance. The objectives of this process are to provide information and facts to the supervisor and to clarify the perception of the employee. Research has indicated that a person tends to overestimate his or her own level of performance (Thornton, 1980). Participation may result in a more realistic perception and may aid communication with the supervisor.

The degree of participation of the employee in the preparation of his or her own performance summary depends on the methods used, the type of job, and the personalities of the employee and supervisor. When management by objective or goal setting is used, the employee prepares a draft of his or her own performance summary. When a standardized rating form is used, such as graphic rating scales, the participation of the employee may be limited to providing information to the supervisor. Employees who are managers or supervisors may participate to a greater degree than those below the supervisor level.

Some supervisors may not encourage or request the participation of employees to avoid misunderstandings and conflict, and some employees simply do not want to participate. However, if misunderstandings and conflict are likely to occur, it is better that they be dealt with at this point in the process than to wait until they become even bigger problems. Some employees may be reluctant to participate simply because they have not been informed or do not understand the purpose, or because they have not participated in the past. It seems likely than any reluctance can be reduced if the purpose is understood, and if the organization makes it clear that participation is expected.

SUPERVISOR PREPARES DRAFT

In Process 3.2, Table 4, the supervisor prepares a draft of the employee's performance summary. The objective of this step is to clarify and document the supervisor's perception of the level of performance of the employee. Inputs to this process include: policies and procedures, the methods and forms to be used, informal appraisals made during the period covered by the summary, feedback given the employee, and information obtained from the employee.

A great deal of effort has been expended over the years to identify sources of error and develop better methods of measuring performance. Nevertheless, it must be recognized that all currently available methods are subject to considerable error. The goal, therefore, is to follow procedures that will minimize error when making formal appraisals of performance (Wexley & Yukl, 1977).

Although the types of human error in performance ratings have been thoroughly researched and documented, the decisions that must be made by the supervisor have received little attention. When preparing formal appraisals the supervisor must make a number of decisions and may be influenced by a number of factors. There may be no one in the work group who has performed in what he or she thinks to be an outstanding manner. Nevertheless, the supervisor may feel that the best performers in his or her work group must be recognized and rewarded if the effectiveness of the group as a whole is to be maintained or improved. Unless the best performers receive some kind of recognition, group members may begin to feel that the supervisor is not looking out for their interests. Further, there may be no incentives to maintain or improve their levels of performance. More than one supervisor has been sorry when no one in his or her work unit received recognition or an award while workers in adjacent work units did.

Another source of error is when the supervisor concludes that the ratings he or she gives may not contribute to group effectiveness unless they are consistent with the perceptions of the members of the work unit. Supervisors try to avoid making decisions that can be interpreted as playing favorites, or unfair and less than honest.

More than a few supervisors feel that all of the members of "their" work unit are head and shoulders above those of other work units. They may express this feeling to the work unit frequently in a conscious or unconscious effort to instill a competitive spirit and improve group effectiveness. In situations where the jobs require higher skills than other units, such a conclusion may be justifiable. However, these feelings may result in inflated performance ratings.

The influence of higher level supervisors can be an important pressure on supervisors when they prepare formal performance ratings. Some supervisors may say what they think the boss wants to hear, or go to some length to support an evaluation given previously. Some supervisors may even give low ratings to conceal their own ineffectiveness or, to be more charitable, to avoid losing good workers to other parts of the organization. On the other hand, if a work group has all average performers, and the supervisor rates them accordingly, the ratings may appear to contain the human error of central tendency.

The point is, procedures are needed that will have the best chance of producing performance ratings that are consistent and comparable, and contain minimum error. Some procedures that have proven effective are: (1) ranking all employees from highest to lowest performers to develop an order-of-merit; (2) dividing the order-of-merit into performance categories such as high, average, and below average (3) identifying and recording the behaviors and outcomes on which these judgments were based; (4) preparing a rating for each employee that is consistent with the rankings given, the performance category assigned, and the behaviors and outcomes identified; and (5) submitting the order-of-merit and performance categories, along with the rating forms for employees, to the second-level supervisor. The order-of-merit divided into performance categories can be used by the second-level supervisor and personnel department to detect human error, but it need not be included in the permanent records of employees.

Unless some such procedures are followed, it seems unlikely that the measures produced by the appraisal system will differentiate between the levels of performance of employees. If the system differentiates between high, average, and below average performers, this information can be used to make management decisions. It may be unwise to try to make finer discriminations using performance ratings (McGregor, 1960).

By using the above procedures, differentiations can be made between the levels of performance of employees within a work group. However, there may still be some difficulty when comparing the levels of performance of employees in different work groups that do not share a supervisor. Although it is generally assumed that such comparisons are necessary, this may not be the case in actual practice. For the most part, measures of performance are used to identify "candidates" for some type of personnel action and to validate other selection criteria (Miner, 1975). They are not very useful when making a final selection from a group of candidates who are all rated in the same performance category. For example, if all candidates for promotion are in the high performance category, the minor differences in performance ratings are not likely to be a valid basis for making the final selection (McGregor, 1960).

The final selection of employees from a group of candidates must be based on criteria that have been validated using performance ratings. These criteria may include: prior experience, seniority, demonstrated skills, education, interview scores, assessment center scores, attitude measures, tardiness, absenteeism, and others. Specific accomplishments, skills, and abilities described in performance summaries may also be used as selection criteria. However, all such measures must be validated as being predictive of future performance. The requirement and procedures for validating selection criteria are discussed further in Chapter 10 (USEEOC, 1974).

When preparing a performance summary it may be necessary for the supervisor to use more than one type of rating form. For example, if MBO or goal setting is used, it may be necessary to complete a second rating form such as a rating scale. One form is necessary for MBO and goal setting to record planned activities and expected results, and the degree to which the employee has carried out the plan and achieved the expected results. A standardized rating scale may be necessary to provide a performance rating that can be compared with those of other employees. The completed forms for MBO and goal setting provide a good basis for providing feedback to employees, but they are not very useful for comparing the performance of different employees. Different things may be measured for different employees and they do not produce numerical scores that can be compared (Oberg, 1972).

SUPERVISOR AND EMPLOYEE DISCUSS PERCEPTIONS

In Process 3.3, Table 4, the supervisor and the employee discuss their perceptions of the level of performance. The objectives of the process are: (1) to offer the employee the opportunity to communicate information to the supervisor that he or she feels is important; (2) to insure that the supervisor has all of the facts before preparing the final performance summary; and (3) to develop a mutual understanding of the two perceptions of the employee's level of performance. The degree that these objectives are achieved depends on the leadership and communication skills of the supervisor and the personality and communication skills of the employee.

Sometimes supervisors are influenced by information obtained from sources of which the employee is unaware. This information may be second- or third-hand, inaccurate, and unfair. Nevertheless, the employee may not be made aware of it or may not be given the opportunity to set the record straight. If the truth were known, it is likely that most supervisors have made judgements and given ratings based on such information, and wished later that they could change them. Also, most employees can remember times when they believe they were unfairly judged based on irrelevant statistics or inaccurate information provided to the supervisor by a third party.

Employees are frequently judged by comparing current statistics with those of previous years. Such comparisons may indicate an improvement or a decline that has nothing to do with the actual performance of the person being judged. Changes in such statistics can be influenced by a large number of factors that are not considered or measured by the organization. For example, supervisors are frequently held responsible for increases in unfavorable statistics that may be caused by a single disgruntled employee. The actions of this employee may be directed to embarrassing the organization or someone higher in the chain of supervision. Nevertheless, the first-level supervisor may still be held responsible.

An example of the inappropriate use of statistics is frequently seen in the military. The commander of a military unit may be held responsible for the personal conduct of the members of the unit when on or off duty. One of the statistics that is frequently used to measure the effectiveness of the commander is the percentage of soldiers who are absent without leave. The percentage for the current month is compared with that of the same month for previous years. The fact that there have been major changes in personnel during the year is frequently overlooked. Experienced and well disciplined soldiers may have been replaced with soldiers who have completed only minimum training and have not yet adjusted to the demands of the military. The fact is, such percentages are seldom comparable because they are measures of the conduct of two different groups of people.

Process 3.3 provides the opportunity for the employee and the supervisor to discuss the information on which perceptions of the level of performance are based before the final judgements are made, and before they are used to determine the future of the employee. The degree that the employee's participation in this process influences the final rating given may depend on a number of factors. These may include: how well the employee states his or her case, the relationship developed between the supervisor and the employee, how sure the supervisor is of his or her own judgments, and a number of other variables. Because of these variables, it is difficult to see how performance ratings can be considered anything but subjective judgments. Nevertheless, judgments of performance should be based on as many relevant objective measures as possible.

SUPERVISOR PREPARES FINAL SUMMARY

In Process 3.4, Table 4, the supervisor prepares the employee's final performance summary based on his or her understanding of the level of performance. The objective of this process is to produce a measure with minimum human and administrative error.

The final performance summary may include both an MBO or goal-setting format and one of the rating scales. Both types of measures may be used for managers and supervisors. Some type of rating scale and an essay appraisal may be used for employees below supervisor level. As previously mentioned, the procedures followed by supervisors can also include ranking employees and placing each employee in either the high, average, or low performance categories.

Completed summaries are then submitted to the second-level supervisor for review.

REVIEW FINAL PERFORMANCE SUMMARY

In Process 3.5, Table 4, the formal summaries of performance are reviewed by the second-level supervisor and the personnel department. The objectives of this process are to provide information to the second-level supervisor and to detect and correct administrative and human error that may have occurred.

By reviewing the appraisals, the second-level supervisor can get a general idea of the status of the work force in his or her department, can determine the ability of the first-level supervisor to appraise performance, and can detect administrative and human error. Types of human error include: leniency, strictness, central tendency, personal bias, or halo effect. Halo effect is the tendency to rate an employee high or low on all factors measured because he or she is considered to be high or low on a single criterion. For example, the supervisor who values self-reliance may give an employee high ratings on all factors measured because he or she judges the employee to be self-reliant.

Usually higher levels of supervisor may not alter or amend a summary prepared by the lower level supervisor. Only when an injustice is obviously being perpetrated should a reviewing supervisor be permitted to alter an appraisal except in cases of administrative error. If a second-level supervisor believes that a measure of performance contains human error or the judgments made are inaccurate, he or she may return the appraisal to the lower level supervisor for further justification or reconsideration. Performance measures should be returned, however, only in special circumstances and with caution. The purpose must be to correct administrative or suspected human error, not to instruct the first-level supervisor how to rate his or her employees. When there is undue pressure or influence exercised by the second-level supervisor, some first-level supervisors may react by saying what they think the boss wants to hear rather than providing an accurate measure of performance.

The second-level supervisor may also be required to record his or her own perceptions of the level of performance of the employee on the same rating form. The ratings given by the first- and second-level supervisors are then averaged. The rationale for averaging is that it tends to reduce the impact of a single, perhaps biased, rating (Miner, 1975). The problem with averaging is, the second-level supervisor may not have the opportunity to obtain first-hand information about the level of performance of employees. If this is so, the rating given by the second-level supervisor may be more of a judgment of the first-level supervisor's ability to appraise performance than a measure of the performance of employees. Instead of reducing biased ratings, the damage can be doubled if the second-level supervisor does not have first-hand knowledge of the employee's performance, and simply agrees with the rating given by the first-level supervisor (Wexley & Yukl, 1977).

After the second-level supervisor has reviewed and signed the appraisal forms, they are forwarded to the personnel department for review. It is at this point in the process that the system breaks down in some organizations. The ratings are often reviewed by a records clerk who does not have the tools or the necessary skills to detect human error. This can happen because many organizations have yet to recognize the need for this special training. Detecting human error can be a relatively simple task if the information needed is recorded in a computer data file, the necessary computer programs are developed, and personnel are trained to use them. It is doubtful, however, if many organizations have developed these tools at the level where they can be most useful. A well trained personnel specialist with the proper tools can detect errors and can advise supervisors how to correct them before appraisals become final (Miner, 1975).

When the personnel specialist has completed his or her review, the appraisal is returned to the first-level supervisor to be used for providing feedback to the employee. If error is detected or suspected, a list of recommendations for correcting the error is also provided to the supervisor by the personnel specialist. It should be made clear, however, that these are only recommendations. The personnel specialist should not be placed in the position, or given the authority, to require supervisors to change an appraisal. The personnel specialist should have the skills to be a confidential advisor to supervisors at all levels on matters pertaining to performance appraisal, but should not be given the power to distort the appraisal process.

CONSEQUENCES OF FAILURE

The consequences of failure resulting from discrepancies in the design or operation of Subsystem 3.0 are listed below. These symptoms or risks of failure are identified by asking the questions: "What if this input is not used?"; "What if this process is not carried out?"; and "What if this objective is not achieved?"

Process 3.1

What if employees do not provide information to supervisors about how they evaluate their own level of performance or if they do not draft their own performance summary?

- Employees can assume an unrealistic level of performance without being faced with objective facts.

- Employees may not be prepared to participate in discussions about their level of performance with the supervisors.

- Employees may not understand or accept the judgments of supervisors.

- Employees may not be prepared to challenge misinformation or unfair and unreasonable judgments made by supervisors.

Process 3.2

What if supervisors do not prepare draft performance summaries for employees before putting them in final form?

- Supervisors may not give the preparation of performance summaries the attention they require.
- The system may not produce valid and reliable measures of performance.
- Measures and judgments of performance made during the appraisal period may not be given due consideration when preparing final performance summaries.
- Performance summaries may not be made in a timely manner.
- Supervisors may not discuss performance summaries with employees before they become final.
- Employees may not have the opportunity to challenge unfair and unreasonable judgments before they become final.

Process 3.3

What if supervisors and employees do not discuss their draft performance summaries before final summaries are prepared?

- Supervisors may make judgments in final summaries that they cannot support with job related behaviors or outcomes.
- Discussions of final performance summaries can become difficult and less constructive.
- Employees may be encouraged and justified in challenging final performance summaries.
- Employees are less likely to accept judgments of less than adequate performance and take actions to improve performance.
- Employees may lose trust in supervisors and consider the appraisal system to be unfair.

Process 3.4

What if supervisors do not prepare final performance summaries?

- Measures of performance will not be available for making management decisions.
- There will be no basis for providing feedback or identifying actions that are necessary to improve performance.
- Employees who deserve recognition and awards may be overlooked for lack of formal measures of performance.
- Employees who should be considered for further training or separation may be overlooked.
- Supervisors may not carry out other necessary supervisory processes.
- Performance ratings will not be available for use in validating selection criteria according to EEOC Guidelines.

Process 3.5

What if second-level supervisors and personnel departments do not review formal performance measures?

- Formal summaries may contain administrative and human error that make them invalid and unusable.
- Second-level supervisors may not receive the information needed to judge the ability of the first-level supervisor to appraise performance.
- Second-level supervisors may not receive all of the available information needed to make personnel decisions and identify training needs.
- Second-level supervisors may not make personnel changes that could improve the work force.

SUMMARY

Subsystem 3.0 of the appraisal system consists of a series of steps to follow when completing and reviewing formal summaries of performance that cover specific periods of time. These steps include: (1) the participation of the employee, (2) the preparation of draft summaries, (3) a discussion of the draft summaries by the employee and supervisor, (4) the preparation of a final summary, and (5) the review of the performance summary by the second-level supervisor and the personnel department. The objectives of this subsystem are to produce formal measures of performance with minimum administrative and human error and to provide the second-level supervisor information about the level of performance of employees.

Most organizations can do a better job of detecting and correcting error in appraisals if performance summaries are prepared for all personnel of a work group at the same time, and personnel specialists are properly trained and provided the necessary conceptual tools for detecting error. Much can be done to reduce error by establishing appropriate procedures to be used by supervisors when preparing formal measures of performance.

REFERENCES

Bernardin, H. J., & Abbott, J. (1985). Predicting (and preventing) differences between self and supervisor appraisals. *Personnel Administrator, 30*(6): 151–157.

Fishback, G. (1972). Appraising office and plant employees. In J. J. Famularo (Ed.), *Handbook of modern personnel administration.* New York: McGraw-Hill, pp. 41–1 to 41–14.

Herrold, K. F. (1972). Principles and techniques of assessment. In J. J. Famularo (Ed.), *Handbook of modern personnel administration.* New York: McGraw-Hill, pp. 40–3 to 40–11.

Kearney, W. J. (1979). Behaviorally anchored rating scales: MBO's missing ingredient. *Personnel Journal, 58*(January): 20–25.

Lopez, F. M., (1968d). Measuring human performance. In *Evaluating employee performance*. Chicago: Public Personnel Association, pp. 163–286.

McGregor, D. (1960). A critique of performance appraisal. In *The human side of enterprise*. New York: McGraw-Hill, pp. 77–89.

Miner, J. B. (1975). Management appraisal: A capsule review and current references. In K. N. Wexley & G. A. Yukl (Eds.), *Organizational behavior and industrial psychology*. New York: Oxford University Press, pp. 382–392.

Oberg, W. (1972). Make performance appraisal relevant. *Harvard Business Review, 50*(1): 61–76.

O'Meara, J. C. (1985). The emerging law of employee's rights to privacy. *Personnel Administrator, 30*(6): 159–165.

Thornton, G. C., III. (1980). Psychometric properties of self-appraisal of job performance. *Personnel Psychology, 33*: 263–271.

U. S. Equal Employment Opportunity Commission (EEOC). (1974). *Affirmative action and equal employment: A guidebook for employers* (Vol. 1). Washington, DC: EEOC.

Wexley, K. N., & Yukl, G. A. (1977). Measuring employee proficiency. In *Organizational behavior and personnel psychology*. Homewood, IL: Richard D. Irwin, Inc., pp. 197–228.

Zedeck, S., & Cascio, W. F. (1982). Performance appraisal decisions as a function of rater training and purpose of the appraisal. *Journal of Applied Psychology, 67*(6): 752–758.

CHAPTER 7

The Performance Review

The fourth step of the typical appraisal strategy is to provide feedback to the employee on the final formal measure of performance produced by the previous step. The performance review or interview has been a subject of debate over the years by researchers and the critics of appraisal. The debate has focused on the practice of showing the performance ratings to employees and the traditional objectives of the review.

Those who have supported the practice of showing ratings to employees have argued that employees have a right to see and appeal or rebut them. Moreover, they must be given the opportunity to see the ratings if trust and confidence in the system is to be maintained. Those who oppose this practice have argued that employees have a right to see and appeal or rebut ratings only when a disciplinary action is being contemplated that might result in separation for substandard performance or improper conduct. Research suggests that supervisors tend to inflate ratings when they know they must show them to employees (Miner, 1975).

In part, this issue has been resolved by legislation and the courts. The Federal Privacy Act of 1973 mandated the creation of the Privacy Protection Study Commission (PPSC) to determine if the act should be applicable to the private sector as well as federal government and federal contractors. In 1977, the PPSC released a report titled, "Personnel Privacy in an Information Society." One of the thirty-four recommendations made was that effective privacy protection policy should allow employees access to records relating to their qualifications for employment, promotion, pay raises, and all documents relating to discipline or discharge. A number of professional personnel associations have urged compliance with these recommendations and privacy legislation has been introduced or enacted in at least fifteen states. The bulk of this legislation would allow employees access to records such as performance ratings. Civil rights legislation has also been interpreted as establishing the right of employees to challenge performance measures when they are used for the purposes of selecting people for hiring or other personnel actions (Wells, 1982).

Beyond the direct legal implications, there are compelling practical reasons for allowing employees access to performance ratings. First is the issue of employee confidence in the fairness of the system; if the results of appraisal are withheld, uncertainty and suspicion may result which would limit the willing participation of employees. Second, if appraisals are to influence performance in a positive way, the results must be communicated. Third, access to results provides an opportunity for an individual to challenge judgments or to correct the simple mistakes that are inevitable in any system. Finally, access to such information is essential if the rights of employees are to be protected (Wells, 1982).

SEPARATING CRITIQUE AND PLANNING

Two of the traditional objectives of the performance review have been to point out areas where the employee could improve his or her performance, and to develop a plan to improve the performance. These objectives have also been the subject of debate over the years.

McGregor (1957) argued that the performance review places the supervisor in two incompatible roles at the same time. In one role the supervisor is to judge and critique performance. In the other role the supervisor is to counsel and assist the employee to improve performance. He considered these two roles to be incompatible because the supervisor could not be a judge and a counselor at the same time. He described the effective counselor to be a neutral party who neither critiques nor praises and whose sole concern is for the health and well-being of the client. McGregor's comments were made in the context of using the "traditional" method of measuring performance. The traditional method at the time was the use of graphic rating scales to measure "traits" which were considered to be characteristics of good performers. To McGregor, the measurement of traits was closer to measuring the personality than the performance of an employee.

Other authorities in the field of performance improvement argued that a supervisor cannot, and should not, be the type of nondirective counselor described by McGregor. They pointed out that it is the job of the supervisor to identify shortcomings and to take some action to improve performance. This cannot be done unless the need for improvement is communicated to the employee (Wells, 1982).

Although these arguments eventually focused on the role of the supervisor, the primary problem was the traditional objectives of the performance review. The critique of performance is likely to generate defensiveness on the part of the employee and may consume the discussion to the point that it is impossible to plan for future performance. Generally speaking, neither the supervisor nor the employee is in the proper frame of mind to plan for the future immediately following a critique of past performance.

To avoid the problem of conflicting objectives, the critique of performance and planning for future performance are separated in the appraisal system described in this book. The critique of performance remains a part of the performance review, but planning for future performance is part of establishing the performance standard in Subsystem 1.0, Chapter 3. The inputs, processes, and objectives of the performance review are shown in Subsystem 4.0, Table 5.

CONDUCT PERFORMANCE REVIEW

In Process 4.1, Table 5, the supervisor and the employee discuss the final formal summary of the employee's performance. The objectives of this process are to: (1) reinforce good performance, (2) identify areas where improvement is needed or can be made, (3) provide incentives for improving poor performance, and (4) permit a verbal appeal or rebuttal.

The role of the supervisor in this process is to provide feedback without animosity, to praise as well as critique, to confront employees constructively, to listen effectively, and to be sensitive to the situations and conditions that employees face (Wells, 1982). If the previous steps of the appraisal process have been carried out, and if the objectives of each step have been achieved, the contents of the final performance summary should be no surprise to the employee. However, if the employee is to be given anything less than the maximum rating, the supervisor must be prepared to explain why in terms of on-the-job behaviors and results.

To reinforce a good performance, the supervisor explains the meaning of the rating given and reviews the job behaviors and results on which the rating is based. If an award or reward is in order, the supervisor may inform the employee that he or she will make such a recommendation. The supervisor should not inform the employee unless he or she is sure that the recommendation will be approved, and that the recognition will be given by the organization.

Regardless of the rating given, the supervisor and the employee should make an effort to identify areas where improvement of performance can be made. For the good performer, this may mean identifying areas where the abilities and skills of the employee are not fully utilized. For the poor performer, this may mean identifying areas where more effort or better skills are needed. For those employees that need increased incentives to improve performance, the supervisor must make it clear that greater efforts are needed on the part of the employee and that he or she will assist the employee in any way possible.

Upon completion of the review, policies and procedures may require that the employee sign the rating form to indicate that the review has been conducted, that the rating is understood, and that the employee understands the right to appeal or submit a rebuttal of the rating.

Table 5
Subsystem 4.0: Conduct Formal Performance Review

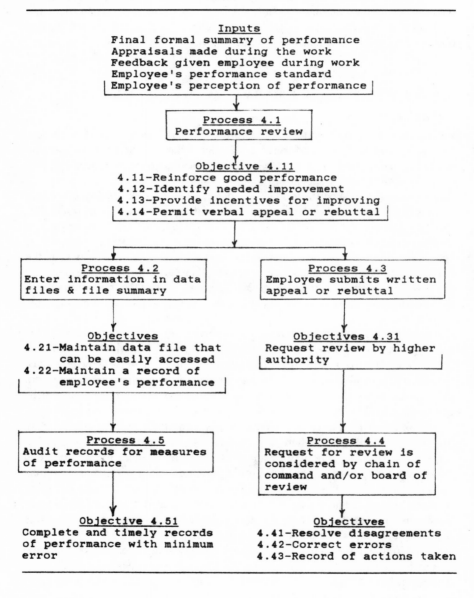

Inputs
Final formal summary of performance
Appraisals made during the work
Feedback given employee during work
Employee's performance standard
Employee's perception of performance

Process 4.1
Performance review

Objective 4.11
4.11-Reinforce good performance
4.12-Identify needed improvement
4.13-Provide incentives for improving
4.14-Permit verbal appeal or rebuttal

Process 4.2
Enter information in data
files & file summary

Process 4.3
Employee submits written
appeal or rebuttal

Objectives
4.21-Maintain data file that
can be easily accessed
4.22-Maintain a record of
employee's performance

Objectives 4.31
Request review by higher
authority

Process 4.5
Audit records for measures
of performance

Process 4.4
Request for review is
considered by chain of
command and/or board of
review

Objective 4.51
Complete and timely records
of performance with minimum
error

Objectives
4.41-Resolve disagreements
4.42-Correct errors
4.43-Record of actions taken

Table 6
Human Resource Functions that Use Performance Measures

Staffing	Rewarding	Developing	Changing
Recruiting	Merit Pay	Job Rotation	Communication
Placement	Rewards	Education	Philosophy
Transfer		Training	Policies
Selecting		Career	Procedures
Promotion		Planning	
Termination			
Skill Inventory			

MAINTAIN DATA FILES

In Process 4.2, Table 5, the personnel department extracts the information needed by other management systems from the performance summary, enters it into a computer data file, and files the formal summary in the employee's personnel records. The objectives of this process are to: (1) maintain a record of information that can be easily accessed and manipulated to meet the needs of management, and (2) maintain a permanent record of the employee's performance.

The data file can be used by the human resource management functions listed in Table 6. These functions use the data file in basically two ways: to identify the high, average, and below average performers; and to validate other criteria that can be used in the selection and development functions. For example, the high performers can be identified as candidates for promotion. However, since all of these candidates will be in the high performance category, other criteria are needed to make the final selections. Other selection criteria usually include: experience, demonstrated skills and knowledge, seniority, test scores, interview scores, education, and other factors that can be found in the personnel records of employees. These criteria must first be entered into the data base, and the necessary calculations made to determine if they are predictive of success in the job to which the person to be promoted will be assigned. If they prove to be valid predictors, they can be used in the final selection process. The minimum standards for validating selection criteria are established by the Equal Employment Opportunity Commission (EEOC) Guidelines. The uses made of the data file when validating selection criteria are discussed further in Chapter 10.

Without the capabilities of a computer, using performance ratings for personnel management decisions is a difficult and time-consuming process. Manual retrieval of the information is necessary as well as complicated statistical analysis by skilled personnel. For this reason, organizations that do not establish automated data files have difficulty validating selection criteria and complying with EEOC Guidelines.

APPEALS AND REBUTTALS

In Process 4.3, Table 5, the employee can submit an appeal for review or a rebuttal of the final summary of performance. The objective is to establish procedures that can be followed by the employee to challenge measures that he or she perceives to be in error or unfair. This process affords the opportunity for employees to influence their futures in the organization instead of having to accept unfavorable reports that would seriously limit their future assignments (Wells, 1982).

REVIEW OF APPEAL OR REBUTTAL

In Process 4.4, Table 5, the appeal or rebuttal of a performance summary is reviewed by successive levels of supervision until the issue is either resolved or it is submitted to the personnel department or a board of review for consideration. The objectives of this process are to resolve disagreements, correct errors or injustices when they occur, and provide a record of review and the actions taken on disagreements. Disagreements should be resolved within the chain of supervision if possible. However, the employee also has the opportunity to have the personnel department or a board of review consider the issue. When necessary, an impartial board of review can be appointed composed of supervisors, employees, and union representatives. The board can also include representation from each of the minority groups in the organization (Wells, 1982).

RECORD AUDITS

In Process 4.5, Table 5, the personnel department audits the personnel records for measures of performance. The objective of this process is to ensure that supervisors and the staff of the personnel department are complying with established policies and procedures for completing and reviewing performance ratings. This process is standard procedure for many organizations. However, follow up actions to correct discrepancies are frequently not carried out. As a result, some supervisors may not take the time or make the effort to complete performance ratings in a timely fashion.

CONSEQUENCES OF FAILURE

The symptoms of failure and the risks to an organization that result from discrepancies in design or operation of Subsystem 4.0 are listed below under the processes in which they are likely to occur.

Process 4.1

What if the supervisor and employee do not discuss the employee's performance rating?

- Good performers may feel their talents are not being recognized.
- Job skills and behaviors that need to be improved may not be identified or understood by the employee.
- Supervisors may not provide rewards for good performance or incentives for improving poor performance.
- The lack of such discussions may result in conflict and may be cited in legal proceedings at a later date.

Process 4.2

What if an automated data file is not maintained and performance measures are not filed in the personnel records?

- Valid and reliable information on performance may not be available for making personnel management decisions.
- Excessive time and effort will be required to retrieve, analyze, and utilize performance information.
- The organization may not use performance as a criterion for recognition and rewards.
- The organization may not validate selection criteria as required by EEOC Guidelines.
- Measures of performance may not be available to justify management decisions when required.

Process 4.3

What if procedures are not established for employees to appeal or rebut performance ratings that they believe to be in error?

- Unfair errors in judgment may go undetected or corrected.
- Employees may feel they have no way of influencing matters that decide their future and they may lose faith in the appraisal process.
- The lack of such procedures may be cited in legal proceedings.

Process 4.4

What if efforts are not made to resolve the disagreements identified in appeals and rebuttals?

- Errors or injustices may occur more often and go undetected.
- Disagreements may not be resolved and will continue to cause conflict and inefficiency.
- Records of actions taken on such disagreements may not be available when required for use in legal proceedings.

Process 4.5

What if the personnel department does not audit the records for performance measures?

- There may be no way of knowing whether policies and procedures for completing performance measures are being implemented.
- It is unlikely that measures of performance will be available for all employees when needed.

SUMMARY

Subsystem 4.0 of appraisal establishes procedures for the review of annual or semiannual performance summaries. The objectives of this subsystem are to: (1) reinforce good performance, (2) identify areas of performance that need improving, (3) maintain an automated data file of performance ratings for use in making management decisions, (4) provide procedures for employees to appeal or rebut performance measures, (5) resolve disagreements generated by performance measures, (6) correct errors or injustices when they occur, (7) maintain a record of review of the actions taken on appeals and rebuttals, and (8) maintain a complete and timely record of the employee's performance while minimizing error.

REFERENCES

Ilgen, D. R., Peterson, R. B., Martin, B. A., & Boeschen, D. A. (1981). Supervisor and subordinate reactions to performance appraisal sessions. *Organizational Behavior and Human Performance, 28*: 311–330.

Ivancevich, J. M. (1982). Subordinates' reactions to performance appraisal interviews: A test of feedback and goal-setting techniques. *Journal of Applied Psychology, 67*(5): 581–587.

Lowe, T. R. (1986). Eight ways to ruin a performance review. *Personnel Journal, 65*(January): 60–62.

McGregor, D. (1957). An uneasy look at performance appraisal. *Harvard Business Review, 35*(3), 89–95.

Miner, J. B. (1975). Management appraisal: A capsule review and current references. In K. N. Wexley & G. A. Yukl (Eds.), *Organizational behavior and industrial psychology*. New York: Oxford University Press, pp. 382–392.

Schick, M. E. (1980). The "refined" performance evaluation monitoring system: Best of both worlds. *Personnel Journal, 59*(January): 47–50.

Webb, D. R. (1972). The computer in personnel administration. In J. J. Famularo (Ed.), *Handbook of modern personnel administration*. New York: McGraw-Hill, pp. 79–1 to 79–13.

Wells, R. G. (1982). Guidelines for effective and defensible performance appraisal. *Personnel Journal, 60*(October): 776–782.

Wight, D. T. (1985). The split role in performance appraisal. *Personnel Administrator, 30*(5): 83–87.

CHAPTER 8

Evaluating the System

Performance appraisal can be described as a dynamic, two-way communication system. Downward communication includes informing employees of the contributions they are expected to make to organizational goals and changes in these expectations as they occur. Upward communication includes information on: (1) how goals can best be achieved, (2) changes that may be needed in expectations and goals, and (3) to what degree goals are being achieved (Lopez, 1968a). The measures of performance produced by the appraisal system are upward communication about how well individual employees are meeting expectations. This information permits the adjustment of expectations and the fair allocation of rewards. But like all communication systems the appraisal system must be maintained continuously, repaired when it breaks down, and updated occasionally to maintain efficiency.

When maintaining the performance appraisal system the practices that need to be maintained must be identified, and determinations must be made about where and why breakdowns are occurring and how to update the system. Managers frequently describe the performance appraisal system as one of their most persistent problems. Reports indicate that managers are seldom satisfied with their appraisal systems, and if they are, it is because of a lack of information about how well it is working. Specific problems that are frequently identified include: a lack of clear objectives, failure to accurately identify what is to be measured, improper selection of measurement methods, and difficulties when providing feedback to employees.

One reason for persistent problems is the lack of system evaluation. To provide a structure for a continuing evaluation effort, Subsystem 5.0 was added to the typical appraisal strategy. The steps of the evaluation procedures include: (1) identifying discrepancies in the system described in the policies and procedures manuals of the organization, (2) documenting the revised system, (3) determining if the system is being carried out in practice, (4) determining if the objectives are being achieved, and (5) determining if the system is producing products that meet the needs of the organization (Provus, 1971). The inputs, processes, and objectives of Subsystem 5.0 are shown in Table 7.

EVALUATING SYSTEM DESIGN

In Process 5.1, Table 7, any discrepancies in the system design of an organization are identified by comparing what is described in the policies and procedures manuals of the organization to the comprehensive system described in Chapters 4 through 8. Tables 2 through 7 identify all of the inputs, processes, and objectives that are necessary for the successful functioning of an appraisal system. An evaluation checklist is provided in Appendix A which is a consolidation of these tables. A design discrepancy exists when a necessary input, process, or objective listed in Appendix A is not adequately described in the documents of the organization. The parts of an appraisal system are linked together in a continuous chain. If a critical part is omitted or not carried out in practice the system is not likely to function effectively.

An organization that is evaluating its system design for the first time is likely to find a number of discrepancies. In many organizations the description of the performance appraisal system is limited to two or three pages in the personnel policies and procedures manual. Other parts of the system are often scattered through a supervisor's manual, an employee guide, or another specialized document. More often than not, necessary parts that are commonly understood as normal duties of a supervisor are not included in any written document. If this is the case, evaluating and communicating the system to the participants would be simplified and improved if the system description is consolidated into one document.

DOCUMENTING THE DESIGN

In Process 5.2, Table 7, the discrepancies identified in policies and procedures are corrected and the entire system is documented. The objectives of this process are to identify and define all of the parts of appraisal that are necessary for the successful functioning of the system and to publish a comprehensive system description that can be used as a guide by the participants.

Many of the problems organizations have with appraisal can be directly attributed to failure to document and to communicate the critical parts to those persons who operate the system. Although verbal instructions may be given on how the system "should" work, participants may not see such instruction as "expectations" of the organization unless they are included in the published policies and procedures. Even if the design is a carefully conceived one, it remains difficult to transfer these insights from the training classroom to the organizational behavior of the work place.

Since most of the tasks of a supervisor are necessary parts of appraisal, the comprehensive description of an appraisal system presented in Chapters 4 through

Table 7
Subsystem 5.0: Evaluate the System

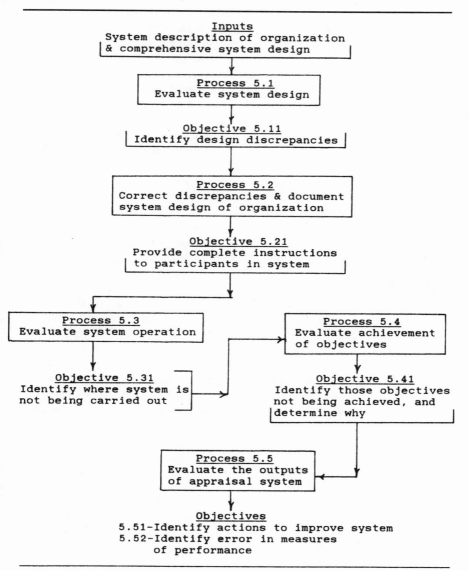

Inputs
System description of organization
& comprehensive system design

Process 5.1
Evaluate system design

Objective 5.11
Identify design discrepancies

Process 5.2
Correct discrepancies & document
system design of organization

Objective 5.21
Provide complete instructions
to participants in system

Process 5.3
Evaluate system operation

Process 5.4
Evaluate achievement
of objectives

Objective 5.31
Identify where system is
not being carried out

Objective 5.41
Identify those objectives
not being achieved, and
determine why

Process 5.5
Evaluate the outputs
of appraisal system

Objectives
5.51-Identify actions to improve system
5.52-Identify error in measures
of performance

8 is a fairly complete list of the supervisor's duties when managing people. The description may seem too complex to be followed by supervisors, but in fact it simply describes what supervisors already do. The design systematizes a supervisor's duties to highlight the important goals of supervisory actions and charts the direction of communication that will improve the functioning of the organization. There is less wasted effort and the truly efficient and beneficial supervisory actions are improved and accentuated. Some supervisors may plan their actions, consider all of the inputs, perform all of their tasks well, and achieve the desired objectives. Others, however, may not plan their actions, may overlook important inputs, may perform their tasks in an unconscious and haphazard way, and fail to achieve any of the objectives of the system. If the system is described in a single document, supervisors will become more familiar with what is expected of them, and can then consciously carry out their tasks in a more deliberate and effective way. If supervisors know that their implementation and managing of the system is to be evaluated, greater efforts will be made to make the system work effectively.

Before changing the system design to correct discrepancies identified in Process 5.1, an organization must decide what changes it wishes to make. A decision can be made that the consequences of failure associated with some part of the system do not warrant changing the system design. A decision can also be made to modify some of the inputs, processes, and objectives of the comprehensive system design to make them more compatible with the existing policies and procedures of the organization. However, any such modifications should be directed to achieving the objectives of the comprehensive design.

Initiating change in organizations can prove to be difficult especially when it involves the performance appraisal system. It may be difficult to convince top management that change is needed. It may be even more difficult to convince those persons who actually operate the system to implement the changes. However, these tasks are made less difficult when the consequences or risks of failure are accurately identified and explained. Knowledge of these risks are crucial to the individual selected to serve in the role of change-agent. By knowing the points of conflict and the mechanics of competing interests he or she can successfully navigate the hazards and substantially reduce the shock of change. The risks an organization takes when there are uncorrected discrepancies are listed at the end of each subsystem in Chapters 4 through 8. The risks are identified for each input, process, and objective of the comprehensive system design.

EVALUATING IMPLEMENTATION

When the system has been corrected, documented, and published it becomes the standard for evaluating the operation of the system.

In Process 5.3, Table 7, information is collected to determine if the processes of the system are being carried out in practice. The objectives are to identify processes that are not being carried out, identify the supervisors who fail to carry them out, and determine why. This requires that information be collected from each part of the organization and analyzed. The sources of this information are supervisors, their employees, and the records produced by the system.

If full cooperation of the participants is to be gained, they must understand the uses to be made of the information they are to provide. If there is fear of being punished in some way for not following policies and procedures, accurate information may be difficult to obtain. Actually, the causes of failure may not be the fault of the participants but may be due to a lack of information about the system, a lack of understanding of what is expected, impractical policies and procedures, or a lack of incentives for carrying them out. There may also be some disagreement with policies and procedures that needs to be identified and resolved. In any case, the solutions to such problems should not include some form of punishment.

Collecting information from all personnel on a continuing basis would be costly and time consuming, and would most likely meet with a great deal of resistance from managers and supervisors. A more practical plan is to select a few personnel from each level and department to participate in each evaluation effort. If the information obtained indicates that there are discrepancies in carrying out the processes, additional efforts can be made to identify specific problems.

The information to be collected is identified from the processes of the system design of the organization. An evaluation checklist is made by stating the processes of the system in question form. The sample checklist shown in Appendix B was made from the processes of the system design described in Chapters 4 through 8. In many organizations it may be necessary to develop lists of more specific questions that can be used in a survey questionnaire. For example, instead of asking supervisors and employees if they carry out the first process by reviewing the inputs to the appraisal system, more information can be obtained if specific questions are asked about each of the inputs.

The necessary information can be collected by conducting personal interviews or by using survey questionnaires. Interviews are conducted by a member of the personnel department who has been given special training. Managers and supervisors can also collect the information from within their own units. It may be, however, that employees are more willing to answer questions honestly and with accuracy if a member of the personnel department conducts the interviews, provided that they can be assured that their answers will be kept confidential. Conducting interviews has the advantage of obtaining information about the degree of concern of the employee, and the interviews offer first-hand knowledge of problems encountered in the operation of the system. The specificity of this direct information is of the sort that might not be collected by the survey questionnaire (Vogel, 1982).

A survey questionnaire can be used, in addition to personnel interviews, to provide a larger sample of information. Managers and supervisors can use a questionnaire within their own units. This has the advantage of getting the persons who operate the system involved in finding ways to make the system work better. A questionnaire can also be used to survey the opinions of random samples of personnel from all work units in each department. If random sampling is used, the participants need not be identified with their answers, and inferential statistics can be used to predict the answers that might have been given if all personnel had been surveyed (Ary, Jacobs, & Razavieh, 1979).

Information obtained from interviews and questionnaires should be tabulated and distributed in such a way that it avoids embarrassment to individuals or specific units. Care must also be taken to avoid the loss of information when making consolidations. With information assembled and sources reassured and protected, corrective actions can and must be taken to eliminate the discrepancies identified. Actions to correct mistakes of individuals and units should be made in confidence and in a way that avoids embarrassment. Otherwise it may be difficult to obtain valid information on a continuing basis.

The symptoms of discrepancies in operation are also useful for identifying the specific point where the system is breaking down and for identifying the risks the organization takes when a necessary process is not carried out in practice. For example, if the appraisal system does not describe the process of identifying the causes of poor performance, or this process is not being carried out in practice, poor performance is likely to continue. Knowledge of the point of breakdown is necessary if changes are to be made that will correct the discrepancy.

DETERMINE IF OBJECTIVES ARE ACHIEVED

In Process 5.4, Table 7, information is collected to determine if the objectives of each of the processes of the appraisal system are being achieved. Although listed as a separate process, it may be possible to collect the necessary information at the same time as for Process 5.3. The sources of the needed information and the techniques used in collecting the information are the same. However, the questions that must be answered are different and more detailed. Checklists to evaluate the achievement of system objectives are made by phrasing each objective in the form of a question. A sample checklist, developed from the objectives of the comprehensive system design described in this book, is provided in Appendix C.

EVALUATE SYSTEM OUTPUTS

In Process 5.5, Table 7, the outputs of the appraisal system are evaluated. There are basically two outputs of the appraisal system. The first is the information obtained from the evaluation of the system. The second output consists of the measures of individual performance produced by the system.

The information obtained from the evaluation of the system is analyzed to determine if changes in the inputs to the system are needed or actions should be taken to correct discrepancies in operation. Discrepancies will occur with varying degrees of importance and judgment must be used to determine what types of difficulties warrant taking action. Individuals will be identified that need assistance, and changes needed to improve the inputs to appraisal may be identified. Assistance might include coaching or providing instruction for a few individuals or providing a training program for all personnel. Since specific problems can be identified, assistance can be tailored to specific needs and costly and unnecessary training can be minimized.

Any part of the system that consistently causes problems, or where objectives are not being achieved, must be examined to determine what changes are needed. Changes in inputs might include revising policies and procedures, revising the method of defining job requirements, or taking actions to change the expectations of the supervisor or other employees for the person assigned to a specific job. Such changes are made by management systems other than appraisal, but the information on which they are based must be provided by the evaluation. For example, when the evaluation of the appraisal system provides information that indicates that some job requirements are poorly designed, they must be revised by an industrial engineer, a job analyst, or a supervisor.

The evaluation of the measures of performance produced by the system entails determining if they meet the needs of the organization. An organization needs measures of performance to: (1) provide feedback to employees, and (2) differentiate between the levels of performance of employees. Procedures for determining if the measures of performance produced satisfy these needs are discussed in Chapter 10.

CONSEQUENCES OF FAILURE

The consequences of failure due to a lack of evaluation in Subsystem 5.0 are listed below. They are general statements which include those listed in the previous chapters. Together these consequences or risks provide justificaiton for initiating a continuous evaluation program for the appraisal system.

Process 5.1

What if the system design of the organization is not evaluated?

- Parts of appraisal may be omitted that are necessary for the successful functioning of the system.
- Ineffective policies and procedures may not be identified and corrected.
- There may not be a valid standard for evaluating the operation of the system.

Process 5.2

What if the apraisal system is not properly documented and communicated to the personnel of the organization?

- Personnel may not understand the system or their responsibilities and tasks in making it work.
- Changes to correct system discrepancies may not be implemented.
- Personnel may consider only the documented portions of the system as mandatory and omit those tasks that are necessary but not outlined in procedures.

Process 5.3

What if no effort is made to determine if policies and procedures are being carried out?

- There may be no way of knowing if the system is or is not working.
- There may be no way of knowing what is wrong if the system is not working.
- Time, effort, and resources will be spent with little or no improvement in operation.

Process 5.4

What if no effort is made to determine if the objectives of the system are being achieved?

- Faulty processes may not be identified.
- Supervisors who have difficulty achieving the objectives may not be identified and given assistance.

Process 5.5

What if the outputs of the appraisal system are not evaluated?

- The appropriate methods for measuring performance may not be used.
- Measures of performance may not provide a suitable basis for providing constructive feedback to employees.
- The system may not produce valid and reliable measures of performance for making management decisions or validating other selection criteria.
- Measures of performance may not distinguish between the levels of performance of different employees.
- Policies and procedures that do not work may not be identified and changed.

SUMMARY

Subsystem 5.0, Table 7, of the comprehensive system design details the structure and procedures for a continuing program of system evaluation. The concept of evaluation includes: (1) evaluating the design to identify and correct discrepancies, (2) determining if the system is being carried out in practice,

(3) determining if the objectives of the system are being achieved, and (4) evaluating the outputs of the system to determine if they meet the needs of the organization.

The comprehensive system description, described in Chapters 4 through 8, is used as the "standard" for evaluating the system design of an organization. A design discrepancy is defined as an input, process, or objective of the standard that has not been described in the documents of an organization. When discrepancies are corrected, the organization's system description is used as the standard for evaluating implementation and the achievement of system objectives.

Evaluating the outputs of the appraisal system is an essential process to determine if the information produced by the system can be used to meet the needs of the organization. Information is needed to provide feedback to employees, to make decisions about personnel, and to identify additional changes that can be made in the system to improve efficiency. Descriptions of the methods used to measure performance and procedures for evaluating measures of performance are provided in Chapters 9 and 10.

REFERENCES

Ary, D., Jacobs, L. C., & Razavieh, A. (1979). *Introduction to research in education* (2nd ed.). New York: Holt, Rinehart, and Winston.

Lopez, F. M. (1968a). Significance of the setting. In *Evaluating employee performance*. Chicago: Public Personnel Association, pp. 43–55.

Mathis, R. L., & Cameron, G. (1981). Auditing personnel practices in smaller-sized organizations: A realistic approach. *Personnel Administrator, 26*(4): 45–49.

McAfee, R. B. (1980). Evaluating the personnel department internal functions. *Personnel, 57*(3): 56–62.

Provus, M. (1971). *Discrepancy evaluation for education program improvement and assessment*. Berkeley, CA: McCutchan.

Vogel, A. (1982). Employee surveys: The risks, the benefits. *Personnel, 59*(1): 65–70.

CHAPTER 9

Methods of Measuring Performance

Over time a number of different methods have been developed for measuring performance. Some of these methods have the potential of generating information that can be successfully used to provide feedback to employees, but do not generate information that can be used to make management decisions. Some methods provide information that can be used for making management decisions, but not for feedback. Still other methods provide information that can be used for both purposes, but make compromises in regard to what is measured and how it is measured which limit their utility. All available methods have advantages and disadvantages, and all are subject to error. As a result, most organizations use combinations of methods to provide measures of performance to meet their needs (Oberg, 1972). The available methods can be divided into four categories based on their similarities. These categories are: (1) narrative summaries, (2) rating scales, (3) checklists, and (4) ranking procedures.

NARRATIVE SUMMARIES

There are five methods of measuring performance that involve the writing of narrative summaries of what an employee did or did not do during the appraisal period. These methods include: essay appraisal, critical incidents, field review, group appraisal, and management by objective (MBO) and goal setting. Each of these methods is described below. Although different formats and procedures are used for each of these methods, the end products are virtually the same. A summary is written at the end of the appraisal period to describe the employee's performance. When using a narrative method a summary can be written in the terms used in the employee's performance standard and observed behaviors and results can be described. If the supervisor has provided feedback to the employee on his or her level of performance during the appraisal period, the contents of the summary will not be a surprise to the employee. For these reasons, narrative summaries can be used successfully for providing feedback (Wexley & Yukl, 1977).

The primary disadvantages of the narrative methods are: they do not provide measures the differentiate between the performance of different employees and they are very vulnerable to human error. Different things may be measured for each employee and they do not produce numerical scores that can be used for comparisons. These methods are vulnerable to human error because the supervisor describes the performance in his or her own words which may be interpreted differently by other people. The words used by one supervisor to describe an above average performance can be interpreted as describing an average performance by another supervisor. Furthermore, the accuracy of some of these methods may depend more on the willingness and ability of the supervisor to express himself or herself in writing than the actual performance of the employee (Wexley & Yukl, 1977).

Essay Appraisal

In the essay method, the first-level supervisor writes a paragraph or more to describe the employee's performance for the period covered by the appraisal. In some organizations the supervisor is free to write whatever he or she feels is important. However, most organizations require supervisors to group comments under headings such as: job performance, reasons for this level of performance, employee characteristics, and development needs.

Essay appraisal was the first method used for the purpose of establishing a permanent record. One of the earliest recorded examples of an essay appraisal is from the files of the U.S. War Department. In 1813, the commander of the 27th Infantry Regiment summarized the performance of his officers. The intent was to provide a record of information that could be used to select officers for future assignments. The general kept his remarks short and to the point: "an ignorant, unoffending Irishman"; "a man whom all unite in speaking ill, a knave despised by all"; and "a good officer but drinks hard and disgraces himself and the service." It seems unlikely that the general's appraisals could be used very successfully for providing feedback, and one wonders what future assignments these officers received (Flanagan, 1982).

If essay appraisals accurately describe observed behaviors and results in the terms used in the work place, they can be very useful for providing feedback. They are also useful for recording specific skills, accomplishments, and short-comings that may not be identified when using other methods. But they may also measure different behaviors for different employees, and they do not produce numerical scores. As a result they are not very useful for identifying candidates for personnel actions or validating other selection criteria. They can, however, be a useful source of information about experiences and skills that can be used, when validated, in making final selections for personnel actions (Miner, 1975).

Critical Incidents

The critical incidents method is primarily a technique for recording incidents that occur during the appraisal period. The supervisor records all incidents of each employee's behavior that result in either unusual success or failure on some aspect of the job. At the end of the appraisal period these incidents are summarized using different formats, but essay appraisal is normally used.

All incidents are recorded in a specially designed book that is divided into general categories of performance. Examples of categories for managers and supervisors include: planning, decision making, delegating, report writing, interpersonal relations, and so on. For hourly workers the categories might include: safety, initiative, cooperation with co-workers, quality and quantity of work, and alertness to problems. Space is provided under each category for recording both negative and positive incidents.

In theory, this method forces the supervisor to observe the performance of each employee, collect factual data on which to base appraisals, and provide timely feedback to employees. In practice, it takes a lot of the supervisor's time and can lead to oversupervision. Employees sometimes feel that their supervisors are keeping "little black books" on them for the purpose of imposing sanctions. There is also evidence that the method does not result in supervisors providing timely feedback. Since the critical incidents method emphasizes record keeping, supervisors often wait until the end of the appraisal period before providing feedback.

The primary advantage of this method is that the information recorded can be used to provide feedback in terms of both specific behaviors and results. It may also identify specific accomplishments, skills, and shortcomings that can be used in making final selections. However, different incidents may be recorded for each employee and the method does not produce numerical scores that can be compared. For these reasons, the method is not very useful for selecting candidates for personnel actions or for validating other selection criteria (Wexley & Yukl, 1977).

Field Review

The field review method derives its name from the procedure of having a representative of the personnel department go into the "field" to assist supervisors in the preparation of performance summaries. The personnel specialist obtains information about each employee's performance by asking supervisors a series of detailed questions and on occasion interviewing employees. He or she then prepares a draft appraisal for each employee. The supervisor reviews the drafts, modifies them as he or she sees fit, and signs the final forms.

The intent of this method is to provide professional assistance, reduce the time required of supervisors, and reduce human error. In theory, human error is reduced by standardizing the meanings assigned to the words used to describe performance, and by eliminating the differences of writing skills of supervisors. However, experience has indicated that field review often serves as an excuse for some supervisors to avoid the responsibility of appraising the performances of their employees. It also raises doubts in the minds of employees as to who is actually doing the appraising. Whether intended or not, the personnel specialist may find himself or herself placed in the position of interpreting the information obtained, judging the degree of performance indiciated, and describing the performance in words that imply success or failure. If supervisors then modify the appraisals written by the personnel specialist, the advantages of standardization are lost (Oberg, 1972).

Group Appraisal

Group appraisal is accomplished by the supervisor directly superior to the employees to be rated and three or four other supervisors. These additional supervisors are carefully chosen for their knowledge of the employees' work and their ability to contribute to discussions about the performance of the employees in general. The group aids the immediate supervisor by discussing the standards of performance for jobs, the current performance of employees, reasons for these levels, and ways to improve performance. The immediate supervisor, or a trained conference leader, coordinates the discussions and is responsible for keeping the discussions as objective as possible. The immediate supervisor is also responsible for preparing the final appraisals. The essay method is normally used to summarize the performance.

Theoretically, the use of multiple judges can cancel out personal bias and other forms of human error. It may be more fair and valid than individual appraisals by the immediate supervisor, and permits the development of an awareness of the degree of human error in appraisals. Group appraisals are useful when there is reason to suspect personal bias, and when some supervisors appear to be using higher or lower standards than others. However, it is time consuming and it is difficult to find supervisors who are familiar enough with the performance of employees to make fair judgments. Group appraisal provides a satisfactory basis for providing feedback to employees, but normally does not produce numerical scores that can be compared (Wexley & Yukl, 1977).

Management by Objective and Goal Setting

Following World War II, standardized graphic rating scales were developed for the purpose of reducing the human error found in essay appraisals and to provide measures that could be used to select personnel for different types of personnel actions. These scales measured personal "traits." Since these traits were considered to be characteristic of all good performers, standardized forms could be developed that measured the same things for most employees in an organization. The scales also produced numerical scores that could be compared.

In the early 1950s, the measurement of traits was severely criticized by a number of authorities in the field of performance improvement. These critics concluded that the "traditional" rating scale placed supervisors in the position of judging the personality and personal worth of employees rather than actually measuring their performance (McGregor, 1957). They argued that supervisors disliked, and frequently avoided, filling out the forms and conducting interviews with employees to provide feedback because they disliked "playing God." The solution proposed by the critcis was to use Drucker's (1954) concept of management by objective (MBO) to appraise performance.

Management by objective and goal-setting techniques are considered by many authorities and practitioners to be methods of management rather than methods of appraisal. Nevertheless, these methods employ the use of a form to record the performance of the employee, and this completed form becomes a part of the permanent records of the employee. Furthermore, these two methods incorporate most of the supervisory processes that are necessary for an appraisal system to function successfully. The MBO and goal-setting methods include the following steps:

1. Top management develops organizational goals and objectives.
2. Department heads develop goals, objectives, and action plans to achieve those of the organization.
3. Supervisors and employees establish unit and individual goals and action plans to achieve those of the department.
4. Frequent reviews are conducted at each level to determine progress, identify and solve problems blocking goal achievement, and to formulate changes in plans when necessary.
5. A final review is conducted by each supervisor and employee to determine the degree that action plans were carried out, which goals and objectives were achieved, and to identify the reasons for those that were not achieved.

In the third step of the process, some type of form is used to record the plan for each employee. This form usually has columns for goals or objectives, action plans, the degree that action plans were carried out, the degree that goals or objectives were achieved, reasons for not achieving what was planned, and areas that need improvement. These columns are filled out during the processes and the completed form becomes part of the permanent records of employees (Carroll & Tosi, 1973).

MBO and goal-setting methods provide a structure for planning and recording the performance standard for employees and they emphasize employee participation in the development of these standards. They also emphasize identifying what is expected of employees in terms of both on-the-job behaviors and results. For this reason the completed form is an excellent basis for providing feedback to the employee.

One drawback of these methods is they do not provide numerical scores that can be used to compare the performance of different employees. What is measured for each employee may be different and the degree of goal achievement may not be comparable. Goals set for one employee may be easier or harder to achieve than those set for another. Experience has shown that it is not easy to set goals, they are difficult to measure for some types of jobs, and they may change rapidly. Supervisors also complain that these methods require too much time and paperwork (Oberg, 1972).

Some organizations add a scale at the bottom of the form which requires the supervisor to give an employee an overall rating. Points along the scale may be defined by adjectives such as: poor, below average, average, excellent, and superior. Because this scale requires the supervisor to indicate a judgment of overall performance, it is highly subjective and vulnerable to human error. It also implies a comparison of the performance of the employee with those of other employees but does so without defining what is being compared.

The current trend is to use a second method, along with MBO and goal setting, to provide measures that can be used to compare the performance of different employees. Some type of rating scale is usually recommended.

RATING SCALES

The first standardized method of measuring performance was the graphic rating scale. These scales measured traits that were considered characteristics of good performers and provided a line under each trait along which the supervisor placed a mark. A rating or score was determined by measuring from the end of the line to the supervisor's mark. Examples of traits include: dependability, initiative, intelligence, loyalty, leadership, and moral courage. Traits were difficult to define, and supervisors and employees interpreted them differently. The judgments required of supervisors made the ratings highly subjective, vulnerable to human error, and especially difficult to explain to employees. Based on the knowledge available to us today, it is evident why the original graphic rating scales failed to provide valid measures that could successfully achieve the objectives of providing feedback or for making management decisions (Wexley & Yukl, 1977).

Even today, some organizations still use graphic scales that measure traits, but most of these have been replaced by newer methods. These include graphic scales that measure behaviors and results and behavioral anchored rating scales (BARS).

Graphic Scales that Measure Behaviors and Outcomes

To improve the validity and reliability of the "traditional" graphic scales, traits were replaced by job dimensions expressed as behaviors and results. Examples of job dimensions expressed in terms of behaviors are: "always gets the job done," "takes appropriate action to solve problems without direction," and "stands up for what he or she believes." Examples of job dimensions expressed as results are: "quality and quantity of work," "maintenance of equipment," "control of waste," "safety," and "timeliness." For many jobs, dimensions can be expressed in more specific terms, but a different form must be developed for each different type of job or a family of similar jobs. For example, it is necessary to measure different behaviors and results for office workers, technicians, supervisors, and maintenance personnel.

The scales along which the supervisor indicates the degree that employees exhibit the desired behaviors or achieve the desired results have been given "anchors." These anchors are qualitative and quantitative measures of the job dimensions. Instead of marking along the line or scale, the supervisor checks one of several boxes that have been labeled with anchors. The anchors may be expressed as numbers, adjectives, or specific behaviors. Examples of numerical anchors might include: bottom 10 percent, in the next 20 percent, middle 40 percent, and so forth. Anchors expressed as adjectives might include: poor, below average, average, above average, and outstanding. Finally, examples of anchors expressed as behaviors are: "does as little as possible," "occasionally must be warned," or "eager to do all that is called for."

Graphic rating scales are useful for providing feedback, selecting candidates for personnel actions, validating selection criteria, and providing information for determining the status of human resources. However, the degree of their utility for these purposes depends entirely on how accurately the job dimensions are defined and the degree of human error that is introduced when supervisors rate employees. The closer the job dimensions describe the behaviors and results included in the performance standards of employees, the more useful they are for providing feedback. If human error can be minimized when the appraisals are made by supervisors, the performance ratings provided by graphic scales are useful for making management decisions and validating selection criteria (Wexley & Yukl, 1977).

Behavioral Anchored Rating Scales (BARS)

Behavioral anchored rating scales were developed in order to make graphic rating scales more acceptable to raters and to reduce human error. One of the assumed advantages of BARS is that they eliminate much of the ambiguity found in other scales by defining the anchors in the rater's own terminology. The raters participate in the development of the scales and it is assumed that this will encourage them to complete ratings more carefully and honestly.

BARS, as do other rating scales, typically measure job dimensions expressed in terms of results or behaviors. The difference is they may have as many as six or seven anchors for each job dimension expressed in terms of behaviors. An example of one job dimension and its behavioral anchors is shown below (Wexley & Yukl, 1977).

Cooperation: the worker's ability to work with others.

7—Would go out of his or her way to help others.

6—Would listen to others before losing his or her temper.

5—Would help others with their work after finishing his or her own.

4—Would tell others who have questions to wait until after work.

3—Would lose temper with others when something goes wrong.

2—Would make big problems out of little ones.

1—Would ride and criticize others constantly.

The behavioral anchors are intended to help supervisors make more exact judgments. The supervisors are asked to select the behaviors that "could be expected" of the employee for each job dimension. Note that observed behaviors are not being measured. This permits the supervisor to select a behavior for each job dimension whether or not he or she has actually observed the employee exhibiting the behavior.

Because the anchors are expressed as job behaviors, they can be used to provide fairly specific feedback to employees. They are of value in assisting employees to understand the behaviors expected of them, and to make clear those behaviors that are considered to be less acceptable. Since the ratings produced by BARS can be expressed in numerical terms, they can be used to compare the performance of employees and for validating other selection criteria. As with other rating scales, however, different forms must be developed for different types of jobs and for different job levels. When jobs are changed, or new jobs are added, new scales must be developed. Recent studies have indicated, however, that a common set of scales can be developed that are applicable to a number of different types of jobs (Goodale & Burke, 1975). If the conclusions of these studies prove to be accurate, considerable time and effort can be saved when developing different formats of BARS.

Procedures for developing BARS. Research has indicated that the degree of usefulness of rating scales depends on the care taken in their development and also the degree of participation of the personnel who will use them. The problem is one of identifying job dimensions and anchors that best describe and measure what employees are expected to do. The procedures for developing BARS are described below. These procedures with minor modifications can be used to develop other types of rating scales such as graphic scales that measure behaviors and results.

The procedures for developing BARS consist of six steps: (1) job dimensions are identified, (2) behavioral anchors are identified, (3) behavioral anchors are allocated to job dimensions, (4) behavioral anchors are assigned values, (5) rating scales are formed, and (6) the completed scales are field tested (Smith & Kendall, 1963).

To identify job dimensions, a group of sueprvisors who will be using the forms to rate employees are asked to identify and define independent dimensions of employee proficiency for a family of jobs. The questions to be answered are: "What must an employee do and achieve on these jobs to be considered proficient?" and "Are these dimensions of proficiency independent or do they measure the same things?" Research has indicated that the final rating form should have no less than five and no more than seven job dimensions.

In the second step, each supervisor of the group identifies several behavioral statements for each job dimension that he or she considers are examples of good, average, and poor performance. The intent is to identify anchors that can be used to measure the degree of proficiency for each dimension.

These behavioral statements are assigned to job dimensions in the third step of the procedures by a second group of supervisors. Each member of this group is given a list of the job dimensions and behavioral statements, and asked to independently assign each behavioral statement to one of the job dimensions. Statements that are not assigned to one of the dimensions by a preestablished percentage of the group of supervisors are discarded in order to reduce ambiguous items and overlapping statements.

Values are then assigned to each behavioral anchor. The supervisors that will be using the rating form are given a booklet and a list of twenty or more behavioral statements for each dimension. Each supervisor is asked to rate each statement by assigning a number on a scale of one to seven. The number one indicates the statement that is an example of poor performance, and seven indicates very good performance. The behavioral statements that are assigned the same values most frequently are retained and the rest are discarded.

The behavioral statements retained are reworded to "expected behaviors," and placed in their correct position on the scale according to the scale value assigned. The end result is a behavioral anchored scale with seven behavioral statements for each job dimension. Spaces are also provided on the rating form to collect the necessary administrative information and the information needed in automated data files for making management decisions. For example, if performance measures are to be used to compute the percentages of high, average, and poor performers in each critical skill, a skill designation will be needed in the data file for each employee.

The completed rating scales are field tested by supervisors who have not participated in their development. These supervisors are given copies of the forms and asked to use them to rate their employees on a test basis. They are also asked to comment on any part of the form that raises questions and to estimate how well the forms worked for them. The measures of performance and comments provided by the test are analyzed for differences of interpretation and human error and are revised accordingly.

Comparisons of Rating Scales

After thirty years of research, it seems that little progress has been made in developing sound alternatives to graphic rating scales. There is evidence, however, that there are advantages to using behavioral anchors rather than simple numbers or adjectives. Although BARS may be slightly superior to other forms of rating scales, the cost in time and effort to develop them may not justify changing from graphic scales.

The graphic scale has come under frequent attack, but it remains the most widely used rating method. In a classic comparison with the more sophisticated forced-choice method, it was proven to be as valid and better than most forced-choice formats described later in this chapter. There may be no need to use anything more complicated than a graphic scale supplemented by a few essay questions (Landy & Farr, 1980).

CHECKLISTS

There are two major types of checklists, "weighted" and "forced-choice." Like rating scales, the rater is typically given a list of behavioral statements for each performance dimension. In this case, however, the supervisor is asked to report if he or she "has" observed the employee exhibit these behaviors. The supervisor does not judge the "goodness" of the employee's behavior or indicate the behavior that the employee "could be expected" to exhibit as when using BARS (Wexley & Yukl, 1977).

Weighted Checklists

A weighted checklist consists of a number of performance dimensions each of which has a list of scaled behaviors for anchors similar to BARS. Each dimension may have as many as ten anchors that describe specific behaviors ranging from exceptional to unacceptable behavior. The supervisor is instructed to read each statement carefully and check those that describe behaviors that he or she has observed the employee doing. Spaces are left blank beside statements that describe behaviors the supervisor has not seen the employee do. Each statement is assigned a scale value, but no weights are shown on the checklist. By using this technique, a supervisor does not know what score he or she is giving the employee. The employee's final score is computed by a personnel specialist by averaging the weights of all items checked.

Considerable time and effort is required to obtain observable behavioral statements that are consistently judged by supervisors across the full range of scale values. A separate checklist may be required for each job or job family.

Weighted checklists are a good basis for providing feedback to employees because observed behaviors are recorded rather than judgments or vague impressions. Supervisors are not, however, able to inform employees of the scores they receive. The scores produced by this method can be used to compare the performance of employees in the same job or family of jobs.

Procedures for developing weighted checklists. The procedures for developing weighted checklists are similar to those used to construct behavioral anchored rating scales. However, more behavioral statements are required for each dimension of performance, and a different scoring system is used. A greater number of behavioral statements is required for each job dimension because, when using the form, supervisors can check only those behaviors that they have "observed employees doing."

To identify behavioral statements for eventual use as anchors, a large number of possible anchors is collected for each job dimension that range from "unusually effective" to "unusually ineffective." These statements are compiled from written comments and interviews with supervisors and the performance standards of employees. Care is taken to solicit observable behaviors rather than such subjective conclusions as, "He has a good attitude." The collected statements are then scaled to establish the degree of proficiency indicated by each.

The scale values or weights assigned to each behavioral statement is determined by having supervisors sort them into a number of categories according to the degree of proficiency indicated. For example, if ten supervisors sort the statements into ten categories ranging from poor to outstanding, the same statement could be sorted into several different categories. Assuming that a particular statement was sorted into category five by six of the ten supervisors, into category four by two supervisors, and into category six by two supervisors; the weight of the statement would be computed as follows: $4 + 4 + 5 + 5 + 5 + 5 + 5 + 5 + 6 + 6 = 50$; $50/10 = 5.0$. The weight of the statement would be 5.0.

The weighted behavioral statements are arranged in random order under each of the job dimensions to which they apply and no weights are shown on the checklist. As many as ten statements might be listed under each job dimension. The instructions for completing the checklist are to check all of the statements that reflect behaviors the supervisor has observed the employee exhibiting in the work place. When the checklist is completed it is field tested and revised as necessary.

Forced-choice Checklists

The forced-choice checklist was specifically developed for the purpose of reducing leniency error. Experiences with other methods have shown that supervisors tend to be lenient when they know that performance ratings will be used to determine the future of employees. As a result, performance ratings may be so inflated that they cannot be used to distinguish between the levels of performance of employees.

In a forced-choice checklist, behavioral statements are arranged in groups of four. A checklist may contain as many as ten to twenty of these groups. In each group of four statements there are two that appear to be favorable and two that appear to be unfavorable. However, one of the favorable and one of the unfavorable statements does not discriminate between the effective and ineffective employee. The supervisor is asked to check the one statement of the four that best describes the performance of the employee, and the one statement of the four that least describes the performance of the employee. The values assigned to these statements are kept from the supervisor and all scoring is done by the personnel department.

Forced-choice checklists must be developed by trained personnel specialists for each job or family of jobs. Their development is costly, and supervisors typically dislike the method because they cannot determine what ratings they are giving employees. Research has indicated that this method may result in less bias and leniency error when compared to graphic scales. It is true, however, that clever raters will always find ways to beat the system. For example, if they wish to give a specific employee a high rating, they simply rate their best performer on the rating form and put their preferred employee's name on the form thereby guaranteeing a high rating.

Since this method produces numerical scores, it provides information that can be used for management decisions; but it is not very useful for providing feedback. Since supervisors do not know what performance ratings they have given, they cannot explain the ratings to employees.

RANKING METHODS

The ranking methods entail making a list of employees, with the most effective employee at the top, and the least effective at the bottom. Rankings are usually made for overall performance, but they can also be used to rank employees on specific performance dimensions. There are basically three methods of ranking employees. They are: alternation ranking, paired comparison, and forced distribution (Wexley & Yukl, 1977).

Alternation ranking and paired comparison are among the best available methods of generating valid order-of-merit lists of employees, especially when two or more supervisors rank the same group of employees and their rankings are averaged. These methods do not, however, provide measures of the amount of differences in performance between individuals. For example, it is not possible to determine the difference between the performance of the first and second name on the list or the last name on the list. For this reason, it is not possible to identify the high, average, and below average performers from alternation ranking and paired comparisons. The forced distribution method forces the supervisor to divide employees into these or similar performance categories.

Alternation Ranking

Using alternation ranking procedures, the supervisor decides which employee is the most effective and which is the least effective in the work group. The most effective employee is listed first in the order-of-merit, and the least effective last. The second-most and second-least effective employees are then identified, and so on. The judgment required of the supervisor is to differentiate between the performance of employees in the middle of the list. If two or more raters can be used who have had an equal opportunity to observe the performance of the employees in the group, an average rank can be computed which may assist in differentiating between employees in the middle. It may also improve the rankings by having each rater rank the employees independently and then re-conciling the differences through discussion.

Paired Comparisons

The paired comparison method involves ranking each possible pair of employees in a work group. Employees are randomly paired in all possible combinations and each pair is listed on a card. Procedures usually call for a personnel specialist to prepare a card for each possible pair of employees. The two names on each card are listed so that the same name does not always appear on top. The cards are then shuffled, and the supervisor decides which employee on each card is the better performer. The personnel specialist then computes the number of times each employee is selected by the supervisor, and lists the employees in the order of the number of times selected. A more accurate ranking may be obtained by using more than one rater. The problem with this method is, of course, the large number of comparisons that must be made when there is a large number of employees in a work group.

Forced Distribution

The objective of the forced distribution method is to divide the employees into a specified number of performance categories. Typically a supervisor is asked to distribute the names of employees into five groups with a predetermined percentage in each group. For example, 10 percent may be placed in the category of poor performers, 20 percent below average, 40 percent average, 20 percent above average, and 10 percent in the high performer category.

Using this method assumed that the frequency of performance ratings within a group will conform to a normal curve. The larger the group, the more likely that this assumption is true. Therefore, this method should be used only when thirty or more employees are to be ranked by a single supervisor. Further, the rankings developed by this method should be considered rough estimates rather than true measures of performance.

The forced distribution method has a number of other opportunities for error. First, the assumption that the frequency of performance ratings will conform to a normal curve may not be valid. Some groups may consist of employees who were all selected because of their high level of skills and performance. Employees in this type of group may all perform above average. Further, when poor performers have been terminated, all groups within an organization will have only satisfactory or above performers. Second, placing employees in such categories implies that there are significant differences in their performance. These differences may not exist. The differences between performance categories are often extremely small and frequently impossible to differentiate. Experience has shown that supervisors have difficulty placing employees in these categories in a way that conforms to the numbers assigned by preestablished percentages. The resulting data on performance may bear little resemblance to reality.

How Rankings Can Be Used

Supervisors need a way of knowing that they are being consistent when completing performance summaries for the members of their work groups. When using rating scales, it is often difficult to make cerrtain that the best performer receives the highest rating and the least effective performer the lowest rating. This is more difficult when performance summaries are completed at different times during the year for the members of a work group. An order-of-merit, developed using a ranking method, can be used as a guide to insure that the ratings given are consistent with the levels of performance within the work group. Using ranking methods also seems to be natural and is easily understood by supervisors. If they help the supervisor to be consistent when completing performance ratings, they may also be useful in reducing some types of human error.

It is not necessary to require supervisors to place preestablished percentages of employees in different performance categories or to make the assumption that the distribution of ratings will conform to a normal curve. An order-of-merit can also be used by a supervisor to divide employees into performance categories without being forced to place a specific number in each category and without using all possible categories.

An order-of-merit divided into performance categories can be useful to the second-level supervisor and the personnel specialist to detect inconsistencies in ratings and narrative descriptions and for detecting human error. However, their use should be limited to these purposes. Including procedures and tools in the process to prevent, detect, and correct errors in performance ratings before they become final is the best way of insuring that they are useful as management tools. They need not become part of the performance rating or be included in the permanent records of employees. The ranking methods are not very useful for comparing the performances of employees in different groups or for providing feedback to employees. Informing employees of their rank within the work group is difficult to explain and can result in friction and conflict.

SUMMARY

The focus of this chapter is to describe the different methods that are used to measure employee performance and the advantages and disadvantages of each. This information is needed when evaluating the measures of performance produced by the appraisal system. Most organizations use a combination of methods to provide the information needed to give feedback to employees and as a basis for management decisions.

The available methods are divided into four categories: (1) narrative methods, (2) rating scales, (3) checklists, and (4) ranking procedures. The narrative methods are described as being useful for providing feedback to employees, but not very useful for making management decisions. Rating scales and some types of checklists are described as being useful for providing feedback and for making management decisions, provided they are properly designed. Ranking procedures are described as being useful as guides when completing performance ratings using other methods and for detecting human error. But they are not very useful for feedback or making management decisions. Procedures for evaluating the methods used by an organization are described in Chapter 10.

REFERENCES

Borman, W. C., & Dunnette, M. D. (1975). Behavior-based versus trait oriented performance ratings: An empirical study. *Journal of Applied Psychology, 60*(5): 561–565.

Carroll, S. J., & Tosi, H. L. (1973). *Management by objective: Application and research.* New York: Macmillan.

Deets, N. R., & Tyler, D. T. (1986). How Xerox improved its performance appraisals. *Personnel Journal, 65*(April): 50–52.

Drucker, P. (1954). *The practice of management.* New York: Harper & Bros.

Dukes, C. W. (1972). Skills inventories and promotion systems. In J. J. Famularo (Ed.), *Handbook of modern personnel administration.* New York: McGraw-Hill, pp. 17-1 to 17–20.

Dunnette, M. D. (1967). Predictors of executive success. In F. R. Wickert & D. E. McFarland (Eds.), *Measuring executive effectiveness.* New York: Appleton, Century, & Crofts, pp. 7–47.

Flanagan, E. M., Jr. (1982). All in the name of efficiency. *Army, 32*(6): 48–50.

Goodale, J. G., & Burke, R. J. (1975). Behaviorally based rating scales need not be job specific. *Journal of Applied Psychology, 60*(3): 389–391.

Gorlin, H. (1982). An overview of corporate personnel practices. *Personnel Journal, 61*(February): 125–130.

Graves, J. P. (1982a). Let's put appraisal back in performance appraisal: Part I. *Personnel Journal, 61*(November): 844–849.

Graves, J. P. (1982b). Let's put appraisal back in performance appraisal: Part II. *Personnel Journal,* 61 (December): 918–923.

Ivancevich, J. M. (1974). Changes in performance in a management by objective program. *Administrative Science Quarterly, 19*(4): 563–574.

Jackson, J. H. (1981). Using management by objective: Case studies of four attempts. *Personnel Administrator, 26*(2): 78–81.

Jacobs, R., Kafry, D., & Zedeck, S. (1980). Expectations of behaviorally anchored rating scales. *Personnel Psychology, 33*: 595–637.

Kane, J. S., & Freeman, K. A. (1986). MBO and performance appraisal: A mixture that's not a solution, Part 1. *Personnel, 63*(12): 26–36.

Kingstrom, P. O., & Bass, A. R. (1981). A critical analysis of studies comparing behaviorally anchored rating scales (BARS) and other rating formats. *Personnel Psychology, 34*: 263–289.

Kornhauser, A. (1962). What are rating scales good for? In T. L. Whisler & S. F. Harper (Eds.), *Performance appraisal research and practices.* New York: Holt, Rinehart, & Winston, pp. 8–12.

Landy, F. J., & Farr, J. L. (1980). Performance rating. *Psychological Bulletin, 87*(1): 72–107.

Latham, G. P., & Wexley, K. N. (1977). Behavioral observation scales for performance appraisal purposes. *Personnel Psychology, 30*(2): 255–268.

Lopez, F. M., Kesselman, G. A., & Lopez, F. E. (1981). An empirical test of trait-oriented job analysis technique. *Personnel Psychology, 34*: 479–502.

McCormick, E. J., & Tiffin, J. (1974). Performance evaluation. In *Industrial psychology* (6th ed.). Englewood Cliffs, NJ: Prentice-Hall, pp. 193–219.

McGregor, D. (1957). An uneasy look at performance appraisal. *Harvard Business Review, 35*(3): 89–95.

Miner, J. B. (1975). Management appraisal: A capsule review and current references. In K. N. Wexley & G. A. Yukl (Eds.), *Organizational behavior and industrial psychology.* New York: Oxford University Press, pp. 382–392.

Oberg, W. (1972). Make performance appraisal relevant. *Harvard Business Review, 50*(1): 61–76.

Plachy, R. J. (1983). Appraisal scales that measure performance outcomes and job results. *Personnel, 60*(3): 57–65.

Ruderman, G. P. (1967). Employee merit rating. In H. B. Maynard (Ed.), *Handbook of business management.* New York: McGraw-Hill, pp. 11–144 to 11–156.

Schwab, D. P., Heneman, H. G., III, & DeCotiis, T. A. (1975). Behavioral anchored rating scales: A review of the literature. *Personnel Psychology, 28*: 549–562.

Smith, P. C., & Kendall, L. M. (1963). Retranslation of expectations: An approach to the construction of unambiguous anchors for rating scales. *Journal of Applied Psychology, 47*(2): 149–155.

Tiffin, J., & McCormick, E. J. (1962). Industrial merit ratings. In T. L. Whisler & S. F. Harper (Eds.), *Performance appraisal research and practices.* New York: Holt, Rinehart, & Winston, pp. 4–7.

Wexley, K. N., & Yukl, G. A. (1977). Measuring employee proficiency. In *Organizational behavior and personnel psychology.* Homewood, IL: Richard D. Irwin, Inc., pp. 197–228.

CHAPTER 10

Evaluating Measures of Performance

The symptoms of failure of performance measures are conflict and misunderstandings between employees and supervisors when providing feedback, excessive numbers of appeals and rebuttals of performance ratings, and ratings that are so inflated that they do not differentiate between the levels of performance of employees. These symptoms can be the result of improper selection of methods or the use of poorly conceived rating instruments that do not measure what employees actually do. Unfortunately, these same symptoms can also be caused by human error when supervisors complete rating forms, failure to train the participants in the appraisal process, lack of communication skills, failure to carry out the steps of the appraisal process, or failure to achieve one or more of the objectives of these processes. Organizations that have changed their methods of measuring performance because of these symptoms have frequently found that the new methods worked no better than the old. Since the true causes of failure were not originally identified by a complete system evaluation, the symptoms continued as well as the structural problems that were the true causes of failure.

Because the symptoms can be misinterpreted, the evaluation of performance measures must be directed to determining if the measures provide the kinds of information needed by the organization. This entails determining what information is needed, if the methods used have the potential of providing this information, if the specific instruments used were designed to measure what they have been presumed to measure, and if the measures produced by the system accurately differentiate between the levels of performance of employees.

Organizations need the information provided by measures of performance to provide feedback to employees, reinforce good performance, and improve poor performance. This information is also needed when selecting personnel for specific personnel actions, and to identify programs and policies that are needed to develop fully the human resources of the organization.

INFORMATION NEEDED FOR FEEDBACK

In theory, the annual or semiannual performance rating is a summary of the appraisals made and the feedback given during the period covered by the rating. At the beginning of the appraisal cycle, a performance standard is established that describes what the employee is expected to do. Informal appraisals are made during the period by the supervisor by comparing observed behaviors and results with the performance standard. When providing feedback during the appraisal period, the terms used should be consistent with those used to describe the performance standard. Generally, the closer these terms are to the behaviors and results, the more the supervisor and the employee will agree on their meaning. Further, there should be a common understanding of what was judged to be good performance and what was judged to be unsatisfactory. If feedback is given in terms other than those used in the work place, there is likely to be misunderstandings and conflict. Therefore, methods that permit the supervisor to measure the same things described in the employee's performance standard are likely to provide the best information for use when providing feedback on the annual or semiannual performance rating. Because performance standards for employees may be different, methods that permit supervisors to appraise different outcomes and behaviors for each employee are usually those best suited for providing feedback.

INFORMATION NEEDED FOR MANAGEMENT DECISIONS

Organizations need information about the performance of their employees in order to make decisions about promotions, merit pay, recognition awards, transfers, layoffs, terminations, career development, training and education, future personnel needs, and the recruiting of new employees. There are basically four different ways that performance measures can be used in making such decisions: (1) to select "candidates" for personnel actions, (2) to validate criteria for making selections from groups of candidates, (3) to validate criteria for screening and selecting persons who have applied for employment with the organization, and (4) as statistics to determine the status of human resources.

Selecting Candidates

Procedures for selecting employees for personnel actions usually involve selecting a group of "candidates," and then making final selections from this group. Groups of candidates for specific personnel actions can be identified by comparing performance ratings. For example, employees with high performance ratings may be selected as candidates for promtoion, merit pay, and recognition rewards. Average performers can be identified as candidates for skill improvement training. Employees with low performance ratings may be identified as candidates for counseling, transfer, layoffs, or termination.

In order for comparisons of performance to be valid, the same performance dimensions must be measured, and the method used must produce numerical scores that differentiate between the levels of performance of employees. Therefore, these comparisons must be limited to employees who do similar jobs for which the same rating form is used.

Other methods of identifying candidates for personnel actions include: supervisor nominations, seniority, peer nominations, and self-nominations through posting and bidding programs. Although these methods are necessary parts of organization policy, they have their unavoidable shortcomings. Nominations may not be based on performance, and persons who should be given consideration because they are high performers may be overlooked simply because they have not been nominated. Nominations are usually made only when a vacancy occurs or when some other event takes place that requires action to be taken. Nominations do not provide information on a regular basis which can be used to identify the need for personnel actions. When performance ratings are not used, supervisors and employees lose their confidence in the system and choose not to participate. Getting promoted in this situation depends more on who a person knows than how he or she performs. Persons who need training or those who should be transferred or terminated can go undetected and continue to perform poorly. Organizations may also have difficulty defending personnel actions that are not based on performance (Gruenfeld, 1975).

Validating Selection Criteria

Performance measures are not very useful when making final selections from groups of candidates who are all rated in the same performance category. For example, measures may not be accurate enough to select the best performer from a group of high performers. Usually the members of a group of candidates have been rated by different supervisors, and a rating given by one may have a very different meaning than an equal rating given by another supervisor. Performance ratings are useful, however, for validating criteria that can be used in making final selections from groups of candidates.

Using performance ratings to validate other criteria involves comparing them with other factors, such as prior experience, test scores, seniority, attitude measures, demonstrated skills, assessment center scores, interview scores, and records of absenteeism and tardiness. These factors can be used as selection criteria if it can be shown that they are predictive of success or failure in the specific job for which the selections are being made (Miner, 1975). Minimum standards for validating selection criteria have been established by the Equal Employment Opportunity Commission (EEOC) Guidelines (USEEOC, 1974). These guidelines apply to any type of criteria that are used to screen or select personnel for all types of personnel actions. Empirical evidence must be obtained by studies employing accepted procedures for determining criterion-related validity, such as those described in "Standards for Educational and Psychological Tests and Manuals."

These procedures require that correlations be made between performance ratings and the other factors obtained from the records of employees who have held the job for which selections are being made. These factors can be considered valid selection criteria if significant relationships can be shown with measures of performance. If there are significant positive relationships, it can be said that persons making high scores on these criteria are likely to perform well in the job. Conversely, persons making low scores are not likely to be successful in the job. If proven valid, measures of these criteria can then be used in the final selection process.

As indicated by the EEOC Guidelines, there is a requirement to validate selection criteria for each type of job or family of jobs within an organization. These computations can be very time consuming if they must be done manually. If, however, the necessary information is stored in automated data files and an appropriate computer program is available, the computations can be made in a matter of minutes.

Screening and Selecting Applicants for Employment

Recruiting personnel from outside of an organization usually entails the screening of a number of applicants to select qualified candidates for job vacancies. A final selection is then made from the group of candidates. The information available to persons making these selections is that which can be gleaned from job applications, résumés, scores on tests administered by the organization, and the results of job interviews. Since the applicants may not have worked for the organization before, their performance ratings on previous jobs are not likely to be available. Also, civil rights legislation has placed limits on what types of information can be legally required on job applications, and also what criteria can be used to screen applicants and make final decisions. In general, information cannot be obtained or used that tends to discriminate because of age, sex, religion, race, or ethnic background. Further, any information used as criteria in screening and selecting applicants must be validated using accepted procedures.

The procedures are the same as those for validating criteria for the selection of employees for specific personnel actions. But the criteria to be validated is limited to what can be legally obtained from job applicants. Therefore, measures of performance and of the criteria from the records of employees are used to identify valid selection criteria. Performance ratings and measures of the same criteria that are obtained from job applications are obtained from the records of employees who have held the job. Correlations are then made to determine if there are relationships between their performance ratings and the information obtained from their records. If significant relationships are indicated, these criteria can be used for screening job applicants and making final selections of personnel. These correlations can be made at the same time as those to validate criteria for making final selections from groups of employees.

Determining the Status of Human Resources

Performance ratings can also be used to provide information about the status of human resources. Status reports can show: (1) the percentages of high, average, and below average performers in each skill group; (2) the number of personnel who need additional training in each skill group; (3) the percentage of ineffectives in the work force; (4) the need to develop specific skills to support future goals; (5) which supervisors tend to give all employees high, average, and low performance ratings; (6) the need to conduct training for supervisors; and (7) the reliability of specific instruments in measuring performance. The specific needs for this type of information depends on the extent that all of the possible personnel management functions are developed in an organization. The degree to which this information is available for use, or is used for these purposes, in turn depends on the capability of retrieval from the files. If the information is placed in a computer data file and personnel are available who are qualified to analyze and interpret the data, this information can be put to many uses.

EVALUATING METHODS

Some methods of measuring performance provide information that can be used for feedback but not management decisions. Some methods provide information that can be used for both purposes. Still other methods provide information that can be used for management decisions but not feedback. Other methods are not very useful for either purpose, but are useful as tools to assist supervisors when preparing performance ratings. Evaluating measurement methods involves determining if those used by an organization have the "potential" for providing the information needed for all of these purposes.

The Potential of Available Methods

The available methods of measuring performance and the uses that can be made of them were discussed in Chapter 9. These methods and their uses are summarized in Table 8. The methods shown as having potential for feedback are those that permit supervisors to describe what employees do or fail to do in terms of specific behaviors and outcomes. Because supervisors can individualize each appraisal when using a narrative method, these are best suited for providing feedback. Rating scales and weighted checklists can be used for providing feedback if they measure the behaviors and outcomes that are expected of employees. Since the same rating scale or weighted checklist is used to measure the performance of different employees, the behaviors and outcomes must be described

Table 8
Potential Uses of Methods of Measuring Performance

Methods of measuring performance	Feedback to employees	Management decisions	Tools for supervisors
Narrative Methods			
Essay appraisal	Yes	No	No
Critical incidents	Yes	No	Yes
Group appraisal	Yes	No	Yes
Field review	Yes	No	Yes
MBO & goal setting	Yes	No	Yes
Rating Scales			
Graphic (traits)	No	Yes	No
Graphic (behaviors and outcomes)	Yes	Yes	No
Behavioral anchored	Yes	Yes	No
Checklists			
Weighted	Yes	Yes	No
Forced-choice	No	Yes	No
Ranking Methods			
Alternation	No	No	Yes
Paired comparisons	No	No	Yes
Forced distribution	No	No	Yes

in general terms. Therefore, the information they provide may not be as useful for feedback as that provided by the narrative methods.

The methods shown in Table 8 as having potential for making management decisions are those that produce numerical scores. These methods are useful for this purpose only if the scores they provide differentiate between the levels of performance of different employees. The degree that they accurately differentiate between the levels of performance of employees depends on the amount of human error they contain.

The ranking methods shown in Table 8 are potential tools for supervisors. Using alternation ranking and paired comparisons, supervisors can develop an order-of-merit for his or her work group. The order-of-merit functions as an additional tool, especially when supervisors are rating employees using another method such as a rating scale, to insure that the best performers receive the highest ratings and the poorest performers the lowest ratings.

The forced distribution method places employees in performance categories. This method usually assumes that the frequency of performance ratings for a group of employees will conform to a normal curve. However, more accurate assumptions can be made to make the forced distribution method more useful. For example, performance ratings can be used to compute a curve that is more representative of the frequency of performance ratings for work groups. This curve can then be used to make accurate inferences regarding the percentage of employees in each performance category. It should be pointed out that, whether or not forced distribution is used, employees are invariably placed in performance categories when making management decisions. If this is not done at the supervisor level, employees will be placed in performance categories by someone else using assumed percentages, and without the knowledge and judgment of the supervisors. For example, a decision may be made to include the top 10 percent of those personnel with the highest performance ratings in a career development program, or the bottom 10 percent may be considered for further training or separation.

Practical Considerations When Selecting Methods

There are certain practical considerations that are very important when evaluating the methods used by organizations. One of these is that different methods may be needed for managers, supervisors, and other employees. For example, MBO or goal-setting methods can be used for managers and supervisors, but rating scales may be more appropriate for employees below the supervisor level.

The methods used should be acceptable to both management and employees. In organizations where the employees are unionized, it is important that unions support both the methods selected and the uses made of the performance measures. The methods should also be as easily administered as possible. A method that monopolizes the time and efforts of supervisors and employees, and which necessitates a large staff to develop and administer, is not appropriate for most organizations (Wexley & Yukl, 1977).

Possible Combinations of Methods

Because of the unique limitations of each of the methods available, most organizations use combinations of methods. A number of different combinations have the potential of providing information for feedback and management decisions, and at the same time serve as tools to assist supervisors. Two of these combinations are shown in Table 9.

In each of these combinations a narrative method is used to generate information that can be used for feedback. MBO, goal setting, and essay appraisal are vehicles for recording specific skills, accomplishments, and observed be-

Table 9
Two Possible Combinations of Methods

Level	Combination A	Combination B
Managers	Essay Appraisal & Graphic Rating Scales	MBO or goal setting & Behavioral Anchored Rating Scales
Supervisors	Essay Appraisal & Graphic Rating Scales	MBO or goal setting & Behavioral Anchored Rating Scales
Other Employees	Essay Appraisal & Graphic Rating Scales	Essay Appraisal & Behavioral Anchored Rating Scales
Within Groups	Alternation or Paired Comparison & Forced Distribution	Alternation or Paired Comparison & Forced Distribution

havior and results that cannot be clearly identified using a standardized method. Rating scales are included in both combinations to measure the same job dimensions for employees holding similar jobs and to provide numerical scores that permit the comparisons necessary when making management decisions.

Ranking methods have been included in both combinations for two reasons. First, ranking methods provide results that can be used by the supervisor to develop an order-of-merit. The order-of-merit is then used as a guide by the supervisor to give consistent performance ratings and to insure that the best performers receive the highest ratings and the poorest performers the lowest ratings. Second, rankings provide valuable data for the second-level supervisor and personnel specialist when reviewing performance ratings for human error. Having supervisors complete rankings is a way of obtaining information that may not be made available when only narrative methods and rating scales are used. Forced distribution is included in both combinations of methods to indicate what meaning the first-level supervisor has assigned to the ratings given employees. The objective is to identify those personnel whose performance is above average, average, and below average. The first-level supervisor should be permitted to omit any of these categories that he or she considers are not appropriate for the work unit, and percentages of personnel to be placed in each category need not be established.

A major difference between the two combinations of methods shown in Table 9 is the amount of time and effort required to develop different formats for each job family and how much time is needed to complete the appraisals themselves.

Combination A uses methods that require less time and effort than those in Combination B. Nevertheless, organizations may have other practical reasons for using those methods listed in Combination B despite the greater expenditure of time and effort. For example, the system of management may be management by objective, and some organizations may find that behavioral anchored rating scales are more acceptable to managers, supervisors, and employees than graphic scales.

Checklist to Evaluate Methods

Evaluating appraisal methods involves determining if those used have the potential for meeting the needs of the organization. Since organizational needs have already been identified in general terms, a checklist of evaluation questions can be developed. These questions are listed below. A more complete list must be developed for organizations who identify more specific needs.

1. Is a narrative method used that permits recording of specific skills, accomplishments, shortcomings, and observed behaviors and outcomes?
2. Is a different rating scale or weighted checklist used for each family of jobs?
3. Are ranking methods used to assist supervisors in giving consistent ratings and to detect human error?
4. Do the methods used minimize the time and effort required of supervisors and the personnel staff?
5. Are the methods used accepted by management and the employees being appraised?
6. Does the union support the methods being used?

EVALUATING MEASURES PRODUCED BY THE SYSTEM

Even though the methods used may be appropriate, the measures of performance produced by the system may not meet the needs of the organization. To determine if they are suitable for providing feedback and if they differentiate between the levels of performance of employees, the measures produced by the system must be evaluated.

Evaluating for Feedback

When developing a single rating form for a family of jobs, dimensions of performance (what is to be measured) must be identified that are common to all of the jobs in the job family. The procedures for identifying and defining these dimensions are described in Chapter 9. The sources of job dimensions are the performance standards of employees. If what is measured by a rating form is not what is described in these performance standards, it is probable that the desired performance will not be reinforced, that areas that need improving will not be identified, and that incentives will not be offered for improving performance. In fact, the rating can even reinforce or cause unsatisfactory performance. Therefore, measures of performance should be evaluated for feedback by comparing what was measured with what is described by performance standards. If there are major differences, the rating forms must be redesigned.

The opinions of supervisors and employees may also be used to evaluate performance measures for feedback. Rating forms that, in the opinion of supervisors and employees, do not measure what the employees do are not likely to be useful for providing feedback. Further, if supervisors and employees have experienced difficulty when feedback is provided, the rating form used may be the cause. Since jobs change frequently, rating forms must be redesigned when they no longer measure what is expected of employees.

Evaluating for Management Decisions

Evaluating measures of performance for management decisions involves determining if they accurately differentiate between the levels of performance of employees. When appropriate methods are used, and care has been taken to develop the specific forms used, the primary threat that remains is human error. Types of human error include: leniency, central tendency, strictness, halo effect, personal bias, the effects of rater characteristics, and the hierarchical distance between the rater and rated.

Leniency, central tendency, and strictness. Some supervisors are reluctant to give high or low ratings to employees. Instead, they tend to give average ratings even though there may be large differences in performance. Others tend to give ratings that are in the upper or lower end of the scale. Such differences cause problems when ratings are compared, particularly when the ratings are prepared by different supervisors. Research has indicated that one of the most frequent errors is leniency. When supervisors know that performance ratings will be used in making personnel decisions there is a reluctance to give low ratings or to record criticisms. As a result, they can become so inflated that there is very little difference between the ratings given the best and poorest performers. Nevertheless, if the above average, average, and below average performers can be identified the ratings can be used for making management decisions. But any attempt to compare specific scores received by employees in the same performance category may be invalid. If proper procedures are followed, however, it may not be necessary to make finer distinctions than high, average, and below average performers; and we may be fooling ourselves when we attempt to make finer distinctions. Performance ratings can only be considered as being approximations of true levels of performance.

Halo effect. Halo effect refers to the tendency of some raters to rate an employee generally high or low because they feel the employee is high or low on a single job dimension. For example, if the supervisor values dependability, he or she may give high ratings on all job dimensions simply because the employee is judged to be dependable.

Personal bias. Personal bias may result from an employee's physical attractiveness, race, ethnic background, seniority, level of education, social standing, reputation, experience, age, personality, and the relative importance of their unit in the organization. Even the best raters may have a tendency to give high ratings to those employees who they perceive to be similar to themselves.

Characteristics of raters. Human error may also be introduced due to characteristics that are inherent in the rater. The research on such characteristics has offered relatively few general conclusions, but some consistent effects have been described. The sex of the rater does not generally effect ratings, although female raters may tend to be more lenient. Raters usually give higher ratings to same-race ratees. However, this may be moderated by the degree of contact that members of different races have with each other. When people of different races become better acquainted there is usually less bias. Rater age and education have been studied too infrequently to make general statements about their effects. It appears that the cognitive complexity of the rater may be an important variable. Research has indicated that the complexity of the thought processes of the rater affects the efficiency of processing and evaluating information. Rater experience appears to have a positive effect on the quality of ratings. But, it is not known whether this is the result of more training, experience in rating, better observation skills, better knowledge of job requirements, or other factors. Production-oriented raters seem to be less lenient and to pay more attention to planning activities than those that are interactive-oriented.

Distance. The accuracy of ratings is often a function of the distance between the rater and the rated. The first-level supervisor can be expected to produce a more accurate rating than a second- or third-level supervisor. Generally the more opportunity the rater has to observe the performance the more accurate the rating. However, the relevance of the rater-ratee interaction is more important than simply the amount of interaction. It is necessary that raters have knowledge of the ratee's performance standard, job behaviors, and performance results to adequately appraise performance.

Identifying Human Error

Including procedures for detecting and controlling human error in the appraisal process is one way of insuring that performance ratings can be used for making management decisions. Specific procedures are needed to detect human error when it occurs. If it can be detected, error can be corrected before it becomes part of the permanent record. Researchers use rather complicated mathematical procedures to identify error in different types of performance ratings. Precise answers are needed for such research. However, the problem of organizations is primarily one of detecting error rather than determining precise amounts. The intent here is to describe simple and practical procedures for detecting error

Table 10
Sample Performance Ratings

Employee	Supervisor				
	#1	#2	#3	#4	#5
1.	100	92	86	100	100
2.	97	92	85	99	98
3.	97	91	85	99	93
4.	96	91	85	99	93
5.	96	90	84	98	93
6.	94	90	84	84	90
7.	94	89	84	83	90
8.	93	89	83	83	85
9.	92	88	82	83	83
10.	91	88	82	82	82
Average –	95	90	84	91	90.7

which do not require complicated computations. The data shown in Table 10 illustrates the use of these procedures.

The columns in this table list the ratings given to fifty different employees by five supervisors using the same rating form. It was assumed that each supervisor rated ten employees, and the maximum possible rating was one hundred. The ratings shown in the table were selected to illustrate different types of human error, and may not be typical of actual ratings found in organizations.

In the form in which the ratings are presented in Table 10 human error is difficult to detect. It becomes more apparent, however, when a frequency distribution is made. A frequency distribution of the same ratings is shown in Table 11. This table was made by counting the frequency that the same rating was given by each supervisor. For example, the first supervisor gave a rating of 100 to one employee, 97 to two employees, and 96 to two employees, and so on.

The numbers in the totals column of this table were computed by adding across the columns of the table. These numbers indicate the number of employees who received the same scores in all five groups. The cumulative total is computed by starting at the top of the totals column and adding the frequency of scores. The dotted line through the table indicates that half of the employees received ratings above the line and half received ratings below the line. In Table 11 there

Table 11
Frequency Distribution of Sample Ratings

Possible Ratings	Supervisors					Frequency of ratings	Cumulative number of ratings
	#1	#2	#3	#4	#5		
100	1			1	1	3	3
99				3		3	6
98				1	1	2	8
97	2					2	10
96	2					2	12
95							
94	2					2	14
93	1				3	4	18
92	1	2				3	21
91	1	2				3	24
- -							
90		2			2	4	28
89		2				2	30
88		2				2	32
87							
86			1			1	33
85			3		1	4	37
84			3	1		4	41
83			1	3	1	5	46
82			2	1	1	4	50
Totals	10	10	10	10	10	50	
Average	95	90	84	91	90.7	90.14	

are actually twenty-four ratings above the line and twenty-six below the line.

The next step of the procedure is to analyze the data in Table 11 for indications of human error. It should be remembered that the same form was used to rate all of the employees, and all employees performed the same or essentially similar jobs. Further, it is assumed that equally capable people have been assigned to each work group. Based on this assumption, the distribution of performance ratings for the five groups of employees should be similar. If necessary, this assumption could be verified by comparing the personnel records of the five groups.

As indicated, all of the ratings given by supervisor number one are above the dotted line. All ten of the employees of this group were rated in the top half of the fifty employees rated. Unless the performance of this work group as a whole was above that of the other work groups, the ratings most likely contain leniency error.

The ratings given by supervisor number two are bunched tightly around the dotted line. These ratings contain the error of central tendency. There is a difference of only four points between the bottom and top ratings given by this supervisor, which contrasts with an average difference of twelve points for the other supervisors.

The ratings given by supervisor number three are all grouped below the dotted line. Unless the performance of this work group as a whole was significantly lower in quantity and quality than the other work groups, these ratings probably contain the error of strictness.

The ratings given by supervisor number four are split into two groups with one group at the top of the distribution and the other at the bottom. This indicates that the ratings contain some form of bias or halo error. A more accurate iden- tification of the particular type of error can be made by further dividing the ratings into categories such as: age, male, female, white, Black, Hispanic, and so forth. If a disproportionate number of high or low ratings are found in one of these categories, the personal bias can be discovered. If a personal bias is not identified, the error may be halo effect.

The ratings given by supervisor number five are distributed throughout the full range of ratings given by the five supervisors and approximate a normal probability curve. Two employees received high ratings, five received ratings in the middle, and three are at the lower end of the distribution scale. Based on this data, there is no indication of error. However, there may be personal bias that cannot be detected. The ratings can only be checked for bias by dividing them into the different bias categories.

The distribution in Table 11 provides clear evidence of human error. It should be kept in mind, however, that such indications cannot be considered conclusive until other possible causes for the imbalance have been investigated. For example, the group that received the highest ratings may have been led to high levels of performance by an outstanding supervisor. Adverse conditions in the work en- vironment may have influenced the performance of the group that received the lowest ratings. An evaluator should investigate all possible causes for an irregular distribution of ratings before concluding that it is the result of human error.

The Effects of Error on Decisions

The limitations placed on the use of performance ratings resulting from human error are illustrated by the data in Table 11. If this distribution were used for making management decisions there could be some very undesirable results produced. For example, assume that the employees in the top 20 percent of the distribution are to be given merit pay, and the employees in the bottom 20 percent are to be terminated. The 20 percent to receive merit pay could be identified by drawing a line across the table under the number ten in the cumulative total column. The ten personnel whose ratings are above the line would receive merit pay. This would mean that no employees who were rated by supervisor number two or three would receive merit pay because their ratings contained errors of central tendency and strictness. On the other hand, eight of the ten employees to receive merit pay would be selected from the groups where the ratings contained leniency error and personal bias or halo effect. If the decision to award merit pay is made based on these ratings it is unlikely that the objective of rewarding the best performers would be achieved.

The 20 percent to be terminated would be identified by drawing a line across Table 11 under the number forty-one in the cumulative total column. The nine employees whose ratings are below the line would be fired. One more employee to be fired would be selected from those whose ratings are immediately above the line. As indicated by the table, no employees would be fired from the groups rated by supervisors number one and two because of the errors of leniency and central tendency. At least seven of the ten employees to be fired would come from the groups rated by supervisors number three and four because of strictness error and personal bias or halo effect. The result would most likely be the loss of faith in the system and management decisions.

Similar problems are encountered when trying to use the data in Table 11 to validate other selection criteria. For example, on-the-job experience usually proves to be a valid selection criteria. This means that the employees with the most experience would, in most cases, receive the higher ratings. However, in this distribution the most experienced employees rated by supervisor number three received lower ratings than the least experienced in group one. Also, the most experienced employees in group two received equal or lower ratings than the least experienced in group one. This assumes, of course, that all groups have equally experienced employees. The best approach to avoiding such statistical anomalies is to detect errors before they become part of the permanent records and to provide assistance to supervisors to correct such errors.

Procedures to Control Human Error

Past efforts to control human error have generally been limited to developing rating methods that are less vulnerable to error and to providing training to raters. Less attention has been focused on detecting and correcting error in ratings before they become a part of the permanent record. In addition to training raters, procedures can be designed to assist raters and reviewers to limit error and to detect and correct it when it occurs. These procedures might include:

1. Rating all employees in the organization for whom the same rating form is used at the same time.
2. Requiring supervisors to:
   • make an order-of-merit using a ranking method,

- divide the order-of-merit into above average, average, and below average performance categories omitting any category that does not apply to the work unit,
- complete the required rating forms so that the ratings given are consistent with the order-of-merit and performance categories, and
- submit the completed rating forms and the order-of-merit divided into performance categories to the second-level supervisor for review.

3. Require second-level supervisors to:
- review the ratings and order-of-merit to insure they are consistent,
- check the rating forms for administrative error,
- make a frequency distribution of the ratings given by all supervisors under his or her control and check for indications of human error,
- return ratings to first-level supervisors for reconsideration when there is administrative error or indications of human error,
- provide coaching and counseling for first-level supervisors on how to avoid human error when necessary, and
- submit the rating forms and order-of-merit to the personnel department when no administrative error or human error can be detected.

4. Require the personnel department to:
- review rating forms for administrative error,
- review ratings and orders-of-merit for each work unit for consistency,
- make a frequency distribution of ratings given by all supervisors for each type of rating form and check for indications of human error,
- return ratings to second-level supervisors for reconsideration when there is administrative error or indications of human error,
- provide information to second-level supervisors to be used in coaching and counseling first-level supervisors, and provide coaching and counseling on how to avoid error as requested,
- return rating forms to the first-level supervisors, through channels, for use in conducting performance reviews when no administrative or human error is detected,
- require first-level supervisors to return the rating forms upon completion of performance reviews, and
- enter the information needed by other management systems in an automated data file, file the rating forms in the personnel records of employees, and maintain a separate file for order-of-merit ratings.

SUMMARY

The primary purpose of this chapter was to describe procedures that can be used by the personnel of an organization to evaluate the measures of performance produced by their appraisal system. These procedures involve determining if the methods used have the potential of providing the types of information needed to provide feedback and make management decisions, and if the actual measures of performance produced by the system can be used for these purposes.

The types of information needed, and the uses that can be made of them, were described. Methods that have the potential of providing this information were identified, as were procedures for evaluating the measures of performance produced by the system. The primary threat to producing usable measures of performance when appropriate methods are used and rating forms are properly designed is described as human error. The different types of human error are enumerated, and simple and practical procedures for detecting human error were discussed.

REFERENCES

Brush, D. H., & Schoenfeldt, L. F. (1980). Identifying managerial potential: An alternative to assessment centers. *Personnel, 57*(3): 68–76.

Cascio, W. F., & Bernardin, H. J. (1981). Implications of performance appraisal litigation for personnel decisions. *Personnel Psychology, 34*: 211–225.

Cook, F. C. (1986). Contaminates of pay for performance. *Personnel, 63*(7): 8–10.

Dertien, M. G. (1981). The accuracy of job evaluation plans. *Personnel Journal, 60*(July): 566–570.

Dhanens, T. P. (1979). Implications of the new EEOC Guidelines. *Personnel, 56*(5): 32–39.

Fombrun, C. J., & Laud, R. L. (1983). Strategic issues in performance appraisal: Theory and practice. *Personnel, 60*(6): 23–31.

Fragner, B. N. (1979). Affirmative action through hiring and promotion: How fast a rate? *Personnel, 56*(6): 67–71.

Friedman, M. G. (1986). 10 steps to objective appraisal. *Personnel Journal, 65*(June): 66–71.

Gardner, W. W. (1972). Personnel statistics. In J. J. Famularo (Ed.), *Handbook of modern personnel administration*. New York: McGraw-Hill, pp. 78–1 to 78–13.

Gruenfeld, E. F. (1975). *Promotion practices, policies, and affirmative action*. Ithaca, NY: Cornell University, New York State School of Industrial Relations.

Hakel, M. D., & Schuh, A. J. (1971). Job applicant attributes judged important across seven diverse occupations. *Personnel Psychology, 24*: 45–52.

Hill, F. S. (1979). The pay-for-performance dilemma. *Personnel, 56*(5): 23–31.

Kleinman, L. S., & Durham, R. L. (1981). Performance appraisal, promotion and the courts: A critical review. *Personnel Psychology, 34*: 103–121.

Korman, A. K. (1971). *Industrial and organizational psychology*. Englewood Cliffs, NJ: Prentice-Hall.

London, M., & Stumpf, S. A. (1983). Effects of candidate characteristics on management promotion decisions: An experimental study. *Personnel Psychology, 36*: 241–259.

Lubben, G. L., Thompson, D. E., & Kasson, C. R. (1980). Performance appraisal: The legal implications of Title VII. *Personnel, 57*(3): 11–21.

Martin, D. C. (1986). Performance appraisal 2: Improving the rater's effectiveness. *Personnel, 63*(8): 28–33.

McCormick, E. J., & Tiffin, J. (1974). Performance evaluation. In *Industrial psychology* (6th ed.). Englewood Cliffs, NJ: Prentice-Hall, pp. 193–219.

McGregor, D. (1964). Can we measure executive performance? *International Management, 19*(6): 59–63.

McGuire, P. J. (1980). Why performance appraisals fail. *Personnel Journal, 59* (September): 744–762.

McMillian, J. D., & Doyel, H. W. (1980). Performance appraisal: Match the tool to the task. *Personnel, 57*(4): 12–20.

Miller, E. C. (1979). Consensus: Pay for performance. *Personnel, 56*(4): 4–11.

Miner, J. B. (1975). Management appraisal: A capsule review and current references. In K. N. Wexley & G. A. Yukl (Eds.), *Organizational behavior and industrial psychology*. New York: Oxford University Press, pp. 382–392.

Mobley, W. H. (1974). The link between MBO and merit compensation. *Personnel Journal, 53*(June): 423–427.

Naffziger, D. W. (1985). BARS, RJPs and recruiting. *Personnel Administrator, 30*(8): 85–96.

Nichols, L. C., & Hudson, J. (1981). Dual-role assessment center: Selection and development. *Personnel Journal, 60*(May): 380–386.

Norton, S. D., Balloun, J. L., & Konstantinovich, B. (1980). The soundness of supervisor ratings as predictors of managerial success. *Personnel Psychology, 33*: 377–388.

Olivas, L. (1980). Using assessment centers for individual and organizational development. *Personnel, 57*(3): 63–67.

Ornati, O. A., & Eisen, M. J. (1981). Are you complying with EEOC's new rules on national origin discrimination? *Personnel, 58*(2): 12–20.

Parisi, A. (1972). Employee terminations. In J. J. Famularo (Ed.), *Handbook of modern personnel administration*. New York: McGraw-Hill, pp. 65–61 to 65–14.

Pitts, R. E., & Thompson, K. (1979). The supervisor's survival guide: Using job behavior to measure employee performance. *Supervisory Management, 24*(1): 23–31.

Polster, H., & Rosen, H. (1974). Use of statistical analysis for performance review. *Personnel Journal, 53*(July): 498–505.

Prien, E. P. (1977). The function of job analysis in content validation. *Personnel Psychology, 30*: 167–174.

Rand, T. M., & Wexley, K. N. (1975). Demonstration of the effect, "Similar to me," in simulated employee interviews. *Psychological Reports, 36*: 535–544.

Schowengerdt, R. N. (1975). How reliable are merit rating techniques? *Personnel Journal, 54*(July): 390–392.

Sweeney, H. J., & Teel, K. S. (1979). A new look at promotion from within. *Personnel Journal, 58*(July): 531–535.

Teel, K. S. (1986). Compensation: Are merit raises really based on merit? *Personnel Journal, 65*(March): 88–99.

Torrence, W. D. (1975). Manpower planning and reduction in force: Competitive status, seniority, and EEOC compliance. *Personnel Journal, 54*(May): 287–289.

U.S. Equal Employment Opportunity Commission (EEOC) (1974). *Affirmative action and equal employment: A guidebook for employers* (Vol. 1). Washington, DC: EEOC.

Wadsworth, G. W., Jr. (1962). Seniority and merit ratings in labor relations. In T. L. Whisler & S. F. Harper (Eds.), *Performance appraisal research and practices*. New York: Holt, Rinehart, & Winston, pp. 55–64.

Wexley, K. N., & Yukl, G. A. (1977). Measuring employee proficiency. In *Organi-*

zational behavior and personnel psychology. Homewood, IL: Richard D. Irwin, Inc., pp. 197–228.

Woltz, W. T. (1980). How to interview supervisor candidates from the ranks. *Personnel, 57*(5): 31–39.

CHAPTER 11

Development Needs

The need to evaluate the design and operation of management systems has been recognized for many years. Most organizations regularly evaluate other types of management systems, but have generally neglected the evaluation of performance appraisal systems and supervision. The primary reason for this neglect has been the lack of a suitable method of evaluation. Managers usually know when they have problems with supervision, but they rarely have a means of identifying exactly what the causes of these problems are. The usual solution is to conduct some type of training and to send managers and supervisors to costly seminars. These activities may address the symptoms, but they are not likely to have a practical effect in an organization unless the true causes of the problems are first identified.

The purpose of this book was to describe a method and procedures that can be used by the personnel of an organization to evaluate their appraisal system and the supervisory processes that are necessary for successful operation. By following these procedures, it is possible to identify the causes of supervisory problems, and identify specific actions that can be taken that will make a difference in an organization. However, some staff agency must be assigned the responsibility for insuring that the procedures are carried out on a continuing basis and to provide the necessary personnel qualified to accomplish the task.

STAFF RESPONSIBILITIES

Conducting a continuous evaluation effort is a full-time job which cannot be accomplished by a junior member of the staff who is assigned the task only as an additional duty. The staff agency given the task of evaluation must have the personnel and the ability to perform the necessary tasks on a regular basis. Most organizations have existing staff agencies that are assigned similar tasks such as training, career counseling, and staff development. These agencies can be assigned this responsibility but must be staffed and trained to carry them out. The evaluation procedures provide new tools that should make this job easier and more effective. In some organizations, however, it might be necessary to organize an entirely new staff agency to carry out the evaluation effort. If the tasks to be performed are clearly defined, the size of the staff agency that is necessary can be determined.

The evaluation procedures and the appraisal system design can be used to identify and define these tasks. Further, each step of the supervisory processes can be analyzed to determine what staff support will be needed to make the system work. An initial list of tasks to be assigned to the staff agency selected or organized should include the following:

- Evaluate the design and operation of the appraisal system.
- Identify and recommend changes to improve the system.
- Document and communicate the appraisal system to all levels of the organization.
- Provide coaching for managers and supervisors on the appraisal of performance and the supervisory processes.
- Identify administrative and human error in performance ratings.
- Conduct reviews of appeals and rebuttals of performance ratings.
- Maintain an automated data file of performance ratings and other information for use in making management decisions.
- Conduct studies to validate criteria for screening and selecting employees and job applicants.
- Conduct studies to generate information about the status of human resources.
- Collect and evaluate information to identify the causes of failure to achieve the objectives of appraisal and supervision.

The tasks listed above are not new ones that have been newly generated by the concept of evaluation. They have been around for a long time. The evaluation procedures simply make it possible to identify the tasks in more precise terms, and to recognize the need to assign them to a staff agency. This need may have been recognized in many organizations, but experience has indicated that the capability to perform them has not been developed at the level where it is needed. Some capability may exist at the corporate level, but personnel departments have had difficulty justifying the need for the tools and personnel with the necessary qualifications that are required. Until recently, the risks an organization takes by not performing these tasks were not clearly recognized and may have seemed acceptable. Today, these risks are important enough to give a higher priority to developing the capability to analyze an organization's system carefully, and to systematically attend to corrective actions.

Developing this capability should not be difficult for most organizations. The evaluation procedures are relatively simple and practical. The primary qualification for an evaluator is that he or she be capable of communicating, coaching, and providing training to supervisors and employees. Using performance ratings to validate personnel selection criteria requires statistical analysis, but this has been a requirement for a number of years. Most organizations have personnel who are skilled in system design and analysis and most have computer sections.

ACTIONS TO CORRECT DISCREPANCIES

The primary objective of a continuing evaluation effort is to identify the specific causes of problems with performance appraisal and supervision. When these causes are known, an organization can target specific actions to solve them. Costly solutions that have little practical impact in the work place can be avoided. Specific actions to correct discrepancies can include the following:

- Change supervisory processes that function ineffectively.
- Revise an objective of a part of the system that is not being achieved.
- Coach supervisors who need assistance.
- Counsel supervisors who commit errors when appraising performance.
- Change the methods of appraising performance, review specific rating forms, and develop new rating forms for new jobs.
- Improve the instructions for completing rating forms.
- Provide training to supervisors on how to use the information produced by the system.
- Provide instruction to managers, supervisors, and employees on how the system is designed and what is expected of them when operating the system.

When taking such actions, it should be recognized that "how" the supervisory processes "should" be carried out by each supervisor depends on a number of variables in the work situation. These variables include: the personalities of the supervisor and the employee, the leadership style of the supervisor, the communicaiton skills of the supervisor and employee, relationships within the work group, the type of job, and other variables that are inherent in an actual work environment. The character of these variables may be different for each possible combination of supervisors and employees. Further, these variables can interact during the appraisal process in a way that produces something less than the desired degree of achievement of objectives. Because of such variables, it may be impossible and undesirable for all supervisors to attempt to carry out the processes in the same way. What works for one supervisor may not work for another, and supervisors can approach problems differently and still achieve the same objectives. Therefore, emphasis should be placed on providing individual assistance to supervisors to identify what approach works best for them.

USES FOR THE SYSTEM DESIGN

The performance appraisal system design presented in this book was developed for use as a standard to which organizations can compare their own appraisal systems. The design provides the structure and tools for continuing evaluation and maintenance of the system. In addition, experience has shown that the design can also be used to plan and conduct training and education programs and to focus research studies on problems that are directly relevant to those of the work place. What follows are brief descriptions of how the system design might be used for these purposes.

Training

A number of organizations have indicated that they can use the system design for: (1) explaining why appraisal is necessary and important, (2) developing training programs, (3) as a tool in supervisor development seminars, (4) as a basis for manuals to be used by company officers for evaluating the appraisal system in their departments, (5) thinking through an appraisal training design and communication processes, (6) as a basic concept for evaluating other personnel systems, and (7) as a management coaching program.

Although the design can be used for these purposes, a well documented description of the organization's system is the most useful document for training purposes. The system of an organization describes what is expected of participants and how their own performance will be appraised. This type of knowledge is directly transferable to the work place. Knowledge presented in training that is not based on the system of the organization is much more difficult to implement. Knowing that all personnel must follow the policies and procedures presented in the training sessions, and that their efforts will be evaluated, should provide more incentives for learning and carrying out the system in practice.

Education

The system design can be more useful as an outline for management courses at the college level. The design outlines a structure for organizing and relating concepts of supervision, leadership, motivation, and research findings to the work place. The separate treatment of these subjects in the past has tended to make it difficult for students to see the interrelationships of the different concepts. The system design can also be used as a detailed flow chart for discussing the issues in supervision, leadership, and appraisal.

Focusing Research

Researchers and the academic community have frequently been accused by managers of developing models and theories that have no practical application in the work place. To some extent, the literature reporting research studies tends to support this criticism. Studies are frequently conducted in a college environment where the variables that can influence the results are different from those found in the work place, and can be more easily controlled. These differences can place severe limitations on the uses that can be made of these studies in organizations. Researchers interested in performance improvement frequently investigate the relationships between broad variables, such as job satisfaction and performance, that are difficult to define and measure. Such studies may be influenced by numerous extraneous variables in the environment that are not identified, measured, or controlled.

The system design described in this book can be used as a tool to focus future research on lesser variables that are more easily defined and measured in the work environment. Based on current knowledge, the system design identifies the necessary processes and the objectives they are intended to achieve. However, new knowledge may change our understanding of these processes, and further explain ''how'' each of them can be carried out to better achieve the objectives. Research might also identify additional inputs, processes, and objectives that will improve the functioning of the system. On the other hand, increased knowledge on the part of the participants may make some of the parts of the system unnecessary. There is little doubt that more emphasis is needed on the discovery of new knowledge that can be used to improve performance appraisal and supervision in the work place. The system design provides a fertile source of research problems and possibilities.

APPENDIX A

Checklist for Evaluating System Design

The purpose of this appendix is to provide a checklist that can be used by the personnel of an organization to evaluate the design of their performance appraisal system. This checklist is a consolidation of the inputs, processes, and objectives of the comprehensive performance appraisal system described in Chapters 4 through 8. It is intended as a convenient guide to assist in identifying the parts of the appraisal system of an organization that may be published in several different documents. The checklist can also be used as an outline to consolidate and publish the description of the appraisal system in one document.

Evaluating the system design of an organization may require searching through such documents as the personnel policies and procedures manual, a supervisor's handbook, an employee guide, and others to determine if each of the critical parts of appraisal is adequately described. A discrepancy exists when a part listed on the checklist is not adequately described in the documents of the organization and made available to the personnel who operate the system. The results of the search of organizational documents are recorded on the checklist by simply checking either the "yes" or "no" column. When a check is made in the "yes" column a separate record should be kept to indicate where the description of the part of appraisal can be found when consolidating the description into one document.

Critical parts of system	Described in published documents?	
	YES	NO

PROCESS 1.1 – Supervisor & employee review
      & exchange perceptions of inputs   ___   ___

  Input 1.11 – Philosophy, policies,
      procedures, and rules   ___   ___

  Input 1.12 – Job requirements   ___   ___

  Input 1.13 – Expectations of supervisors &
      others   ___   ___

  Input 1.14 – Employee's abilities, wants, &
      needs   ___   ___

  Input 1.15 – Methods & formats used to rate
      performance   ___   ___

  Input 1.16 – Knowledge of level of performance
      of employee   ___   ___

  Objective 1.11 – Mutual understanding of
      perceptions of inputs   ___   ___

PROCESS 1.2 – Supervisor develops a tentative   ___   ___
      performance standard for the employee

  Objective 1.21 – A description of the role   ___   ___
      the employee is expected to play

PROCESS 1.3 - Employee develops own tentative   ____   ____

        performance standard

  Objective 1.31 - A description of how the   ____   ____

        employee sees his/her role in the

        organization

PROCESS 1.4 - Supervisor & employee resolve   ____   ____

        differences in descriptions

  Objective 1.41 - A standard by which the   ____   ____

        employee's performance will be judged

  Objective 1.42 - A mutual understanding of   ____   ____

        the employee's performance standard

  Objective 1.43 - Congruence of role & employee   ____   ____

        expectations to extent possible

PROCESS 2.1 - The supervisor coaches the   ____   ____

        employee and both measure performance

  Objective 2.11 - Insure that the standard is   ____   ____

        understood, obtain measures of

        performance, and assists the employee

PROCESS 2.2 - The supervisor compares observed   ____   ____

        performance with the employee's

        performance standard

  Objective 2.21 - A decision that observed   ____   ____

        performance **was** or **was not** up

        to the performance standard

PROCESS 2.3 - The supervisor informs the   ___   ___
            employee that his/her performance
            was up to standard and of the basis
            on which the decision was made
    Objective 2.31 - To reinforce good performance ___   ___
            and keep the employee informed of the
            factors considered in appraisals
PROCESS 2.4 - The supervisor & employee identify ___   ___
            the cause of poor performance
    Objective 2.41 - A decision that the cause of ___   ___
            poor performance was or was not
            within the control of the employee
PROCESS 2.5 - The supervisor corrects   ___   ___
            deficiencies that are outside of
            the control of the employee &
            informs employee of the actions taken
    Objective 2.51 - To remove blocks to good   ___   ___
            performance, maintain the confidence
            of the employee, and reinforce good
            performance when appropriate
PROCESS 2.6 - The supervisor and employee   ___   ___
            identify actions necessary to
            improve performance when the cause
            of poor performance is within the
            control of employee

Objective 2.61 - Provide incentives
      to improve performance

PROCESS 3.1 - The employee provides
      information to the supervisor,
      and may draft his/her own
      performance summary

Objective 3.11 - Clarify the employee's
      perception of his/her level of
      performance, & provide facts to
      the supervisor

PROCESS 3.2 - The supervisor drafts a formal
      summary of the employee's performance

Objective 3.21 - Clarify and document the
      supervisor's perception of the
      employee's level of performance

PROCESS 3.3 - The supervisor and employee
      discuss their two perceptions of the
      level of performance of the employee

Objective 3.31 - Insure that the supervisor
      has all of the pertinent facts

Objective 3.32 - Provide the employee the
      opportunity to describe his/her
      perception of the level of performance

Objective 3.33 - Permit the supervisor to
      understand the perception of the employee

PROCESS 3.4 - The supervisor prepares the   ___   ___
          final formal summary of performance

  Objective 3.41 - Formal measure of the   ___   ___
          employee's performance with
          minimum error

PROCESS 3.5 - The second-level supervisor   ___   ___
          and the personnel department
          review the performance summary

  Objective 3.51 - Provide information to the   ___   ___
          second-level supervisor about the
          performance of employees

  Objective 3.52 - Identify administrative and   ___   ___
          human error

PROCESS 4.1 - The supervisor & employee   ___   ___
          discuss the final formal summary
          of the employee's performance

  Objective 4.11 - Reinforce good performance   ___   ___

  Objective 4.12 - Identify areas of needed   ___   ___
          improvement

  Objective 4.13 - Provide incentives for   ___   ___
          improving performance

  Objective 4.14 - Provide the employee the   ___   ___
          opportunity to appeal or rebut
          the final formal appraisal

PROCESS 4.2 - The personnel department extracts   ___   ___
            the information needed by other
            management systems, enters it into
            an automated data file, and files
            the formal summary in the employee's
            personnel records

   Objective 4.21 - Maintain an automated   ___   ___
            data file that can be easily accessed

   Objective 4.22 - Maintain a permanent   ___   ___
            record of the employee's performance

PROCESS 4.3 - Employee submits written appeal   ___   ___
            or rebuttal

   Objective 4.31 - Provide procedures for   ___   ___
            the employees to submit an appeal
            or rebuttal when they feel that
            performance summaries are in error

PROCESS 4.4 - An appeal or rebuttal is considered ___   ___
            by successive levels of supervision
            until resolved, or until submitted to a
            board of review

   Objective 4.41 - Resolve disagreements when   ___   ___
            they occur

   Objective 4.42 - Correct errors and   ___   ___
            injustices

Objective 4.43 - Provide a record of   ____   ____

    review & actions taken

PROCESS 4.5 - Personnel department audits the   ____   ____

    records for measures of performance

Objective 4.51 - Complete and timely records   ____   ____

    of performance with minimum error

PROCESS 5.1 - Compare system description of the   ____   ____

    organization to the inputs,

    processes, and objectives of the

    comprehensive system design

Objective 5.11 - Identify discrepancies in   ____   ____

    policies and procedures of the

    organization

PROCESS 5.2 - Correct discrepancies in the   ____   ____

    system design and publish revised

    policies & procedures

Objective 5.21 - Include all of the critical   ____   ____

    parts of an appraisal system in

    policies and procedures, and provide

    participants with a complete

    description of the system

PROCESS 5.3 - Determine if policies and   ____   ____

    procedures are being carried out

    in practice

Objective 5.31 - Identify where failure   ___   ___

            to carry out the system is occurring

PROCESS 5.4 - Determine if the objectives of the   ___   ___

            system ar . being achieved

Objective 5.41 - Iaentify those objectives   ___   ___

            that are not being achieved and,

            determine why

PROCESS 5.5 - Evaluate the outputs of the   ___   ___

            appraisal system

Objective 5.51 - Identify actions needed to   ___   ___

            improve design & operation

Objective 5.52 - Identify discrepancies in   ___   ___

            system outputs

APPENDIX B

Checklist for Evaluating Implementation

The purpose of this appendix is to provide an example of a checklist that can be used to determine if the steps of the appraisal system are being carried out in practice. The checklist is a consolidation of the processes of the comprehensive system design described in Chapters 4 through 8. Organizations should develop similar checklists using the processes of their own system design after it has been evaluated, revised, and published.

The checklist can then be used by supervisors as a guide, by managers to determine if the steps of appraisal are being carried out in their departments, and by personnel specialists to evaluate the implementation of the system in the organization. To collect the information necessary to answer the questions on the checklist, it may be necessary to develop a more specific list of questions and separate questionnaires for supervisors and their employees. Supervisors and their employees may have different perceptions of how the steps of appraisal are being carried out.

Steps of the appraisal system (system processes)	Carried out in practice?	
	YES	NO

1.1 - Supervisor & employee review & exchange perceptions of the inputs   ___ ___

1.2 - Supervisor develops a tentative performance standard for the employee   ___ ___

1.3 - Employee develops own tentative performance standard   ___ ___

1.4 - Supervisor & employee resolve differences in descriptions of performance standard   ___ ___

2.1 - The supervisor coaches the employee and both measure performance   ___ ___

2.2 - The supervisor compares observed performance with the employee's performance standard   ___ ___

2.3 - The supervisor informs the employee that his/her performance was up to standard   ___ ___

2.4 - The supervisor & employee identify the cause of poor performance   ___ ___

2.5 - The supervisor corrects deficiencies that are outside of the control of the employee & informs employee of the actions taken   ___ ___

2.6 - The supervisor and employee identify   ___   ___
      actions necessary to improve performance
      when the cause of poor performance is
      within the control of the employee

3.1 - The employee provides information to the   ___   ___
      supervisor about his/her level of
      performance, and may draft own performance
      summary

3.2 - The supervisor drafts a formal summary   ___   ___
      of the employee's performance

3.3 - The supervisor & employee discuss their   ___   ___
      two perceptions of the level of performance
      of the employee

3.4 - The supervisor prepares the final formal   ___   ___
      summary of performance

3.5 - The second-level supervisor and the   ___   ___
      personnel department review the performance
      summary

4.1 - The supervisor & employee discuss the   ___   ___
      final performance summary of the employee

4.2 - The personnel department extracts the   ___   ___
      information needed by other management
      systems, enters it into an automated data
      file, and files the formal summary in the
      employee's personnel records

4.3 - The employee may submit an appeal or a   ____   ____
      rebuttal of the formal measure of
      performance

4.4 - An appeal or rebuttal is considered by   ____   ____
      successive levels of supervision until
      resolved, or until submitted to a board
      of review

4.5 - The personnel department audits the   ____   ____
      records for measures of performance

5.1 - Compare the system description of the   ____   ____
      organization to the inputs, processes,
      and objectives of the comprehensive
      system design

5.2 - Correct discrepancies in the system   ____   ____
      design and publish revised policies
      and procedures

5.3 - Determine if policies and procedures   ____   ____
      are being carried out in practice

5.4 - Determine if the objectives of the   ____   ____
      system are being achieved

5.5 - Evaluate the outputs of the appraisal
      system

APPENDIX C

Checklist for Evaluating Achievement of Objectives

The purpose of this appendix is to provide a sample checklist that can be used by supervisors, managers, and personnel specialists to determine if the objectives of the appraisal system are being achieved. The checklist is a consolidation of the objectives of each of the steps of the appraisal system. Organizations should develop similar checklists using their own system design.

To collect the information needed to answer the questions on the checklist, it may be necessary to develop more specific questions and separate questionnaires for supervisors and their employees. For example, to determine if the supervisor and employee have the same understanding of the employee's performance standard, it will be necessary to ask both to describe the standard and then compare the two descriptions. For other objectives, the information needed can be collected by using a survey questionnaire.

Critical objectives	Is objective being achieved?	
	YES	NO

Process 1.1 - Supervisor & employee review &
      exchange perceptions of inputs

  Objective 1.11 - Mutual understanding of   ___   ___
      perceptions

Process 1.2 - Supervisor develops a tentative
      performance standard for the employee

  Objective 1.21 - A description of the role   ___   ___
      the employee is expected to play

Process 1.3 - Employee develops own tentative
      performance standard

  Objective 1.31 - A description of how the   ___   ___
      employee sees his/her role in the
      organization

Process 1.4 - Supervisor & employee resolve
      differences in descriptions of
      performance standard

  Objective 1.41 - The standard by which the   ___   ___
      employee's performance will be judged

  Objective 1.42 - A mutual understanding of   ___   ___
      the employee's performance standard

Objective 1.43 - Congruence of role & employee ___   ___
    expectations to extent possible

Process 2.1 - The supervisor coaches the employee
    and both measure performance

Objective 2.11 - Insure that the standard is ___   ___
    understood, obtain measures of
    performance, and assist employee

Process 2.2 - The supervisor compares observed
    performance with the employee's
    performance standard

Objective 2.21 - A decision that observed ___   ___
    performance was or was not up to
    standard

Process 2.3 - The supervisor informs the employee
    that his/her performance was up to
    standard and of the basis on which
    the decision was made

Objective 2.31 - To reinforce good performance ___   ___
    and keep the employee informed of
    the factors considered in appraisals

Process 2.4 - The supervisor & employee identify
    causes of poor performance

Objective 2.41 - A decision that the cause ___   ___
    of poor performance was or was not
    within the control of the employee

Process 2.5 - The supervisor corrects deficiencies
        that are outside of the control of
        the employee & informs employee of
        actions taken

  Objective 2.51 - To remove blocks to good   ___   ___
        performance, maintain the
        confidence of the employee, and
        reinforce good performance when
        appropriate

Process 2.6 - The supervisor and employee
        identify actions necessary to
        improve performance when the cause
        of poor performance is within the
        control of employee

  Objective 2.61 - Provide incentives to   ___   ___
        improve performance

Process 3.1 - The employee provides information
        to the supervisor, and may draft own
        performance summary

  Objective 3.11 - Clarify the employee's   ___   ___
        perception of his/her level of
        performance, & provide facts to the
        supervisor

<u>Process 3.2</u> - The supervisor drafts a formal

summary of the employee's performance

   Objective 3.21 - Clarify and document   ___   ___

supervisor's perception of the

employee's level of performance

<u>Process 3.3</u> - The supervisor and employee

discuss their two perceptions of the

level of performance of the employee

   Objective 3.31 - Insure that the supervisor   ___   ___

has all of the pertinent facts

   Objective 3.32 - Provide the employee the   ___   ___

opportunity to describe his/her

perception of the level of performance

   Objective 3.33 - Permit the supervisor to   ___   ___

understand the perception of the employee

<u>Process 3.4</u> - The supervisor prepares the final

formal summary of performance

   Objective 3.41 - Formal measures of the   ___   ___

employee's performance with minimum

error

<u>Process 3.5</u> - The second-level supervisor and

the personnel department review the

performance summary

Objective 3.51 - Provide information to the   ___   ___
          second-level supervisor about the
          performance of employees

Objective 3.52 - Produce measures of   ___   ___
          performance with minimum administrative
          and human error

Process 4.1 - The supervisor & employee discuss
          the final formal summary of the
          employee's performance

Objective 4.11 - Reinforce good performance   ___   ___

Objective 4.12 - Identify areas of needed   ___   ___
          improvement

Objective 4.13 - Provide incentives for   ___   ___
          improving performance

 Objective 4.14 - Provide the employee the   ___   ___
          opportunity to appeal or rebut the
          final formal appraisal

Process 4.2 - The personnel department extracts the
          information needed by other management
          systems, enters it into an automated data
          file, and files the formal summary in the
          employee's personnel records

Objective 4.21 - Maintain an automated data   ___   ___
          file that can be easily accessed

Objective 4.22 - Maintain a permanent   ___   ___

    record of the employee's performance

Process 4.3 - The employee may submit an appeal

    or rebuttal of the formal measure of

    performance

Objective 4.31 - Provide procedures for the   ___   ___

    employee to submit an appeal or

    rebuttal when they feel that

    performance summaries are in error

Process 4.4 - An appeal or rebuttal is considered

    by successive levels of supervision until

    resolved, or until submitted to a board of

    review

Objective 4.41 - Resolve disagreements when   ___   ___

    they occur

Objective 4.42 - Correct errors and injustices ___   ___

Objective 4.43 - Provide a record of review &   ___   ___

    actions taken on appeals & rebuttals

Process 4.5 - Personnel department audits the

    records for measures of performance

Objective 4.51 - Complete and timely records   ___   ___

    of performance

<u>Process 5.1</u> - Compare system description of the
organization to the inputs, processes,
and objectives of the comprehensive
system design

Objective 5.11 - Identify discrepancies in   ____   ____
policies and procedures of the
organization

<u>Process 5.2</u> - Correct discrepancies in the system
design and publish revised policies
and procedures

Objective 5.21 - Include all of the critical   ____   ____
parts of an appraisal system in
policies and procedures, and provide
participants with a complete description
of the system

<u>Process 5.3</u> - Determine if policies and
procedures are being carried out

Objective 5.31 - Identify where failure to   ____   ____
carry out the system is occurring

<u>Process 5.4</u> - Determine if the objectives of
the system are being achieved

Objective 5.41 - Identify objectives that   ____   ____
are not being achieved

<u>Process 5.5</u> - Evaluate the outputs of the

 appraisal system

 Objective 5.51 - Identify actions that can ___ ___

  be taken to improve the design &

  operation of the system

 Objective 5.52 - Identify discrepancies in ___ ___

  the measures of performance produced

  by the system

Bibliography

Armenakis, A. A., Field, H. S., & Mosley, D. C. (1975). Evaluation guidelines for the OD practitioner. *Personnel Journal, 54*(January): 99–103.

Ary, D., Jacobs, L. C., & Razavieh, A. (1979). *Introduction to research in education* (2nd ed.). New York: Holt, Rinehart, and Winston.

Benford, R. J. (1981). Found: The key to excellent performance. *Personnel, 58*(3): 68–77.

Bernardin, H. J., & Abbott, J. (1985). Predicting (and preventing) differences between self and supervisor appraisals. *Personnel Administrator, 30*(6): 151–157.

Bernardin, H. J., & Klatt, L. A. (1985). Managerial appraisal systems: Has practice caught up to the state of the art? *Personnel Administrator, 30*(11): 79–86.

Boles, H. W., & Davenport, J. A. (1975a). Role expectations. In *Introduction to educational leadership*. New York: Harper and Row, pp. 21–43.

Boles, H. W., & Davenport, J. A. (1975b). Leaders and expectations. In *Introduction to educational leadership*. New York: Harper and Row, pp. 44–63.

Borman, W. C., & Dunnette, M. D. (1975). Behavior-based versus trait oriented performance ratings: An empirical study. *Journal of Applied Psychology, 60*(5): 561–565.

Brethower, D. M. (1982). The total performance system. In R. M. O'Brien, A. M. Dickinson, & M. P. Roscow (Eds.), *Industrial behavior modification: A management handbook*. New York: Pergamon Press, pp. 350–369.

Brinkerhoff, R. O. (1980). Evaluation of inservice programs. *Teacher Education and Special Education, 3*(3): 27–38.

Brush, D. H., & Schoenfeldt, L. F. (1980). Identifying managerial potential: An alternative to assessment centers. *Personnel, 57*(3): 68–76.

Carroll, S. J., & Tosi, H. L. (1973). *Management by objective: Application and research*. New York: Macmillan.

Cascio, W. F., & Bernardin, H. J. (1981). Implications of performance appraisal litigation for personnel decisions. *Personnel Psychology, 34*: 211–225.

Catalanello, R. F., & Hooper, J. A. (1981). Managerial appraisal. *Personnel Administrator, 26*(9): 75–81.

Cocheu, T. (1986). Performance appraisal: A case in point. *Personnel Journal, 65*(September): 48–55.

Cook, F. C. (1986). Contaminates of pay for performance. *Personnel, 63*(7): 8–10.

Davidson, J. P. (1981). Communicating company objectives. *Personnel Journal, 60*(April): 479–493.

Deets, N. R., & Tyler, D. T. (1986). How Xerox improved its performance appraisals. *Personnel Jouranl, 65*(April): 50–52.

Delamontagne, R. P., & Weitzul, J. B. (1980). Performance alignment: The fine art of the perfect fit. *Personnel Journal, 59*(February): 115–117.

Dertien, M. G. (1981). The accuracy of job evaluation plans. *Personnel Journal, 60*(July): 566–570.

Dhanens, T. P. (1979). Implications of the new EEOC Guidelines. *Personnel, 56*(5): 32–39.

Dickinson, A. M., & O'Brien, R. M. (1982). Performance measurement and evaluation. In R. M. O'Brien, A. M. Dickinson, & M. P. Roscow (Eds.), *Industrial behavior modification: A management handbook.* New York: Pergamon Press, pp. 51–64.

Dipboye, R. L., & de Pontbriand, R. (1981). Correlates of employee reactions to performance appraisals and appraisal systems. *Journal of Applied Psychology, 66*(2): 248–251.

Dossett, D. L., Latham, G. P., & Mitchell, T. R. (1979). Effects of assigned versus participatively set goals, knowledge of results, and individual differences on employee behavior when goal difficulty is held constant. *Journal of Applied Psychology, 64*(3): 291–298.

Drucker, P. (1954). *The practice of management.* New York: Harper & Bros.

Dukes, C. W. (1972). Skills inventories and promotion systems. In J. J. Famularo (Ed.), *Handbook of modern personnel administration.* New York: McGraw-Hill, pp. 17–1 to 17–20.

Dunnette, M. D. (1967). Predictors of executive success. In F. R. Wickert & D. E. McFarland (Eds.), *Measuring executive effectiveness.* New York: Appleton, Century, & Crofts, pp. 7–47.

Echles, R. W., Carmichael, R. L., & Sarchet, B. R. (1974a). Counseling, giving orders, introducing change, and conducting meetings. In *Essentials of management for first-line supervisors.* New York: John Wiley & Sons, pp. 430–456.

Echles, R. W., Carmichael, R. L., & Sarchet, B. R. (1974b). Performance appraisal, promotions, and compensation. In *Essentials of management for first-line supervisors.* New York: John Wiley & Sons, pp. 459–492.

Feldman, J. M. (1981). Beyond attribution theory: Cognitive processes in performance appraisal. *Journal of Applied Psychology, 66*(2): 127–148.

Fishback, G. (1972). Appraising office and plant employees. In J. J. Famularo (Ed.), *Handbook of modern personnel administration.* New York: McGraw-Hill, pp. 41–1 to 41–14.

Flanagan, E. M., Jr. (1982). All in the name of efficiency. *Army, 32*(6): 48–50.

Fombrun, C. J., & Laud, R. L. (1983). Strategic issues in performance appraisal: Theory and practice. *Personnel, 60*(6): 23–31.

Fournies, F. F. (1973). *Management performance appraisal: A national study.* Somerville, NJ: F. F. Fournies Associates.

Fragner, B. N. (1979). Affirmative action through hiring and promotion: How fast a rate? *Personnel, 56*(6): 67–71.

Fraser, D. (March 1984). Straight talk from a union leader. *Reader's Digest,* pp. 85–88.

Friedman, M. G. (1986). 10 steps to objective appraisal. *Personnel Journal, 65*(June): 66–71.

Gardner, W. W. (1972). Personnel statistics. In J. J. Famularo (Ed.), *Handbook of modern personnel administration*. New York: McGraw-Hill, pp. 78–1 to 78–13.

Gellerman, S. W. (1972). Motivation and performance. In J. J. Famularo (Ed.), *Handbook of modern personnel administration*. New York: McGraw-Hill, pp. 2–1 to 2–7.

Getzels, J. W., & Guba, E. G. (1957). Social behavior and the administrative process. *School Review, 65*(4): 423–441.

Goodale, J. G., & Burke, R. J. (1975). Behaviorally based rating scales need not be job specific. *Journal of Applied Psychology, 60*(3): 389–391.

Gomez-Mejia, L. R., Page, R. C., & Tornov, W. W. (1985). Improving the effectiveness of performance appraisal. *Personnel Administrator, 30*(1): 74–80.

Gorlin, H. (1982). An overview of corporate personnel practices. *Personnel Journal, 61*(February): 125–130.

Graves, J. P. (1982a). Let's put appraisal back in performance appraisal: Part I. *Personnel Journal, 61*(November): 844–849.

Graves, J. P. (1982b). Let's put appraisal back in performance appraisal: Part II. *Personnel Journal, 61*(December): 918–923.

Grayson, C. J. (1979). Management science and business practice. In *Harvard Business Review on Human Relations*. New York: Harper and Row Publishers, pp. 59–70.

Gruenfeld, E. F. (1975). *Promotion practices, policies, and affirmative action*. Ithaca, NY: Cornell University, New York State School of Industrial Relations.

Hakel, M. D., & Schuh, A. J. (1971). Job applicant attributes judged important across seven diverse occupations. *Personnel Psychology, 24*: 45–52.

Haynes, M. G. (1978). Developing an appraisal program. *Personnel Journal, 57*(January): 14–19.

Herrold, K. F. (1972). Principles and techniques of assessment. In J. J. Famularo (Ed.), *Handbook of modern personnel administration*. New York: McGraw-Hill, pp. 40–3 to 40–11.

Herzberg, F. (1968). One more time: How do you motivate employees? *Harvard Business Review, 46*(1): 53–62.

Herzberg, F., Mausner, B., & Snyderman, B. (1959). *The motivation to work*. New York: John Wiley & Sons.

Hill, F. S. (1979). The pay-for-performance dilemma. *Personnel, 56*(5): 23–31.

Holley, W. H., Field, H. S., & Barnett, N. J. (1976). Analyzing performance appraisal systems: An empirical study. *Personnel Journal, 55*(September): 457–463.

Holley, W. H., & Field, H. S. (1982). Will your performance appraisal system hold up in court? *Personnel, 59*(1): 59–64.

Ilgen, D. R., Fisher, C. D., & Taylor, M. S. (1979). Consequences of individual feedback on behavior in organizations. *Journal of Applied Psychology, 64*(4): 349–371.

Ilgen, D. R., Peterson, R. B., Martin, B. A., & Boeschen, D. A. (1981). Supervisor and subordinate reactions to performance appraisal sessions. *Organizational Behavior and Human Performance, 28*: 311–330.

Ivancevich, J. M. (1974). Changes in performance in a management by objective program. *Administrative Science Quarterly, 19*(4): 563–574.

Ivancevich, J. M. (1982). Subordinates' reactions to performance appraisal interviews:

A test of feedback and goal-setting techniques. *Journal of Applied Psychology, 67*(5): 581–587.

Iwanicki, E. F. (1981). Contract plans: A professional growth-oriented approach to evaluating teacher performance. In J. Millman (Ed.), *Handbook of teacher evaluation.* Beverly Hills, CA: Sage, pp. 203–228.

Jackson, J. H. (1981). Using management by objective: Case studies of four attempts. *Personnel Administrator, 26*(2): 78–81.

Jackson, S. E., & Zedeck, S. (1982). Explaining performance variability: Conditions of goal setting, task characteristics, and evaluation contexts. *Journal of Applied Psychology, 67*(6): 759–768.

Jacobs, R., Kafry, D., & Zedeck, S. (1980). Expectations of behaviorally anchored rating scales. *Personnel Psychology, 33*: 595–637.

Jacobson, B., & Kaye, B. L. (1986). Career development and performance appraisal: It takes two to tango. *Personnel, 63*(1): 26–32.

Kane, J. S., & Freeman, K. A. (1986). MBO and performance appraisal: A mixture that's not a solution, Part 1. *Personnel, 63*(12): 26–36.

Kaye, B. L., & Krantz, S. (1982). Preparing employees: The missing link in performance appraisal training. *Personnel, 59*(3): 23–29.

Kearney, W. J. (1979). Behaviorally anchored rating scales: MBO's missing ingredient. *Personnel Journal, 58*(January): 20–25.

Kellogg, M. S. (1965a). The coaching appraisal. In *What to do about performance appraisal.* New York: American Management Association, pp. 31–41.

Kellogg, M. S. (1965b). Before discussing the coaching appraisal. In *What to do about performance appraisal.* New York: American Management Association, pp. 43–52.

Kellogg, M. S. (1965c). Applying the coaching appraisal. In *What to do about performance appraisal.* New York: American Management Association, pp. 53–67.

Kellogg, M. S. (1965d). Work planning and progress review. In *What to do about performance appraisal.* New York: American Management Association, pp. 68–82.

Kellogg, M. S. (1965e). What about personality? In *What to do about performance appraisal.* New York: American Management Association, pp. 83–93.

Kingstrom, P. O., & Bass, A. R. (1981). A critical analysis of studies comparing behaviorally anchored rating scales (BARS) and other rating formats. *Personnel Psychology, 34*: 263–289.

Kleinman, L. S., & Durham, R. L. (1981). Performance appraisal, promotion and the courts: A critical review. *Personnel Psychology, 34*: 103–121.

Korman, A. K. (1971). *Industrial and organizational psychology.* Englewood Cliffs, NJ: Prentice-Hall.

Kornhauser, A. (1962). What are rating scales good for? In T. L. Whisler & S. F. Harper (Eds.), *Performance appraisal research and practices.* New York: Holt, Rinehart, & Winston, pp. 8–12.

Landy, F. J., & Farr, J. L. (1980). Performance rating. *Psychological Bulletin, 87*(1): 72–107.

Latham, G. P., & Wexley, K. N. (1977). Behavioral observation scales for performance appraisal purposes. *Personnel Psychology, 30*(2): 255–268.

Latham, G. P., & Yukl, G. A. (1975). A review of research on the application of goal setting in organizations. *Academy of Management Journal, 18*(12): 824–845.

Lawler, E. E., III, & Porter, L. W. (1967). The effect of performance on job satisfaction. *Industrial Relations, 10*(7): 20–28.

Leonard, W. P. (1962). *The management audit: An appraisal of management methods and performance.* Englewood Cliffs, NJ: Prentice-Hall.

Levine, H. Z. (1983). Consensus: Efforts to improve productivity. *Personnel, 60*(1): 4–10.

Levinson, H. (1979). Appraisal of what performance? In Harvard Business Review (Eds.), *Harvard Business Review on Human Relations.* New York: Harper & Row, pp. 280–292.

Linenberger, P., & Keaveny, T. J. (1981). Performance appraisal standards used by the courts. *Personnel Administrator, 26*(5): 89–95.

Lloyd, W. F., Jr. (1977). Performance appraisal: A shortsighted approach for installing a workable program. *Personnel Journal, 56*(September): 446–450.

Locker, A. H., & Teel, K. S. (1977). Performance appraisal: A survey of current practices. *Personnel Journal, 56*(September): 245–257.

London, M., & Stumpf, S. A. (1983). Effects of candidate characteristics on management promotion decisions: An experimental study. *Personnel Psychology, 36*: 241–259.

Lopez, F. M. (1968a). Significance of the setting. In *Evaluating employee performance.* Chicago: Public Personnel Association, pp. 43–55.

Lopez, F. M. (1968b). Awareness and growth. In *Evaluating employee performance.* Chicago: Public Personnel Association, pp. 81–113.

Lopez, F. M. (1968c). Program review and renewal. In *Evaluating employee performance.* Chicago: Public Personnel Association, pp. 143–158.

Lopez, F. M. (1968d). Measuring human performance. In *Evaluating employee performance.* Chicago: Public Personnel Association, pp. 163–286.

Lopez, F. M., Kesselman, G. A., & Lopez, F. E. (1981). An empirical test of trait-oriented job analysis technique. *Personnel Psychology, 34*: 479–502.

Lowe, T. R. (1986). Eight ways to ruin a performance review. *Personnel Journal, 65*(January): 60–62.

Lubben, G. L., Thompson, D. E., & Kasson, C. R. (1980). Performance appraisal: The legal implications of Title VII. *Personnel, 57*(3): 11–21.

Luthans, F., Maciag, W. S., & Rosenkrantz, S. A. (1983). O. B. Mod: Meeting the productivity challenge with human resource management. *Personnel, 60*(2): 28–36.

Macher, K. (1986). The politics of organizations. *Personnel Journal, 65*(February): 80–84.

Mager, R. F., & Pipe, P. (1970). *Analyzing performance problems or "you really oughta wanna."* Belmont, CA: Fearon Publishers.

Martin, D. C. (1986). Performance appraisal 2: Improving the rater's effectiveness. *Personnel, 63*(8): 28–33.

Maslow, A. H. (1954). *Motivation and personality.* New York: Harper & Row.

Matejka, J. K., Ashworth, D. N., & Dodd-McCue, D. (1986). Managing difficult employees: Challenge or curse? *Personnel, 63*(7): 43–46.

Mathis, R. L., & Cameron, G. (1981). Auditing personnel practices in smaller-sized organizations: A realistic approach. *Personnel Administrator, 26*(4): 45–49.

McAfee, R. B. (1980). Evaluating the personnel department internal functions. *Personnel, 57*(3): 56–62.

McAfee, R. B. (1981). Performance appraisal: Whose function? *Personnel Journal, 60*(April): 298–299.

McCormick, E. J., & Tiffin, J. (1974). Performance evaluation. In *Industrial psychology* (6th ed.). Englewood Cliffs, NJ: Prentice-Hall, pp. 193–219.

McFarland, R. A. (1971). Understanding fatigue in modern life. *Ergonomics, 14*(1): 1–10.

McGregor, D. (1957). An uneasy look at performance appraisal. *Harvard Business Review, 35*(3): 89–95.

McGregor, D. (1960). A critique of performance appraisal. In *The human side of enterprise*. New York: McGraw-Hill, pp. 77–89.

McGregor, D. (1964). Can we measure executive performance? *International Management, 19*(6): 59–63.

McGuire, P. J. (1980). Why performance appraisals fail. *Personnel Journal, 59*(September): 744–762.

McMasters, J. B. (1979). Designing an appraisal system that is fair and accurate. *Personnel Journal, 58*(January): 38–40.

McMillian, J. D., & Doyel, H. W. (1980). Performance appraisal: Match the tool to the task. *Personnel, 57*(4): 12–20.

Meyer, H. H., Kay, E., & French, J. R. P., Jr. (1965). Split roles in performance appraisal. *Harvard Business Review, 43*(1): 123–129.

Miller, E. C. (1979). Consensus: Pay for performance. *Personnel, 56*(4): 4–11.

Miller, E. C., & Steinbrecher, D. D. (1979). Roundup: The ten commandments of "valid" performance appraisal. *Personnel, 56*(5): 45–48.

Miner, J. B. (1975). Management appraisal: A capsule review and current references. In K. N. Wexley & G. A. Yukl (Eds.), *Organizational behavior and industrial psychology*. New York: Oxford University Press, pp. 382–392.

Mischkind, L. A. (1986). Is employee morale hidden behind statistics? *Personnel Journal, 65*(February): 74–79.

Mobley, W. H. (1974). The link between MBO and merit compensation. *Personnel Journal, 53*(June): 423–427.

Morano, R. A. (1974). A new concept in personnel development and employee relations. *Personnel Journal, 53*(August): 606–611.

Mount, M. K. (1983). Comparisons of managerial and employee satisfaction with a performance appraisal system. *Personnel Psychology, 36*: 99–109.

Naffziger, D. W. (1985). BARS, RJPs and recruiting. *Personnel Administrator, 30*(8): 85–96.

Nichols, L. C., & Hudson, J. (1981). Dual-role assessment center: Selection and development. *Personnel Journal, 60*(May): 380–386.

Norton, S. D., Balloun, J. L., & Konstantinovich, B. (1980). The soundness of supervisor ratings as predictors of managerial success. *Personnel Psychology, 33*: 377–388.

Oberg, W. (1972). Make performance appraisal relevant. *Harvard Business Review, 50*(1): 61–76.

Odiorne, G. S. (1972). Evaluating the personnel program. In J. J. Famularo (Ed.), *Handbook of modern personnel administration*. New York: McGraw-Hill, pp. 8–1 to 8–14.

Olivas, L. (1980). Using assessment centers for individual and organizational development. *Personnel, 57*(3): 63–67.

O'Meara, J. C. (1985). The emerging law of employee's rights to privacy. *Personnel Administrator, 30*(6): 159–165.

Ornati, O. A., & Eisen, M. J. (1981). Are you complying with EEOC's new rules on national origin discrimination? *Personnel, 58*(2): 12–20.

Parisi, A. (1972). Employee terminations. In J. J. Famularo (Ed.), *Handbook of modern personnel administration*. New York: McGraw-Hill, pp. 65–1 to 65–14.

Pitts, R. E., & Thompson, K. (1979). The supervisors's survival guide: Using job behavior to measure employee performance. *Supervisory Management, 24*(1): 23–31.

Plachy, R. J. (1983). Appraisal scales that measure performance outcomes and job results. *Personnel, 60*(3): 57–65.

Polster, H., & Rosen, H. S. (1974). Use of statistical analysis for performance review. *Personnel Journal, 53*(July): 498–505.

Prien, E. P. (1977). The function of job analysis in content validation. *Personnel Psychology, 30*: 167–174.

Provus, M. (1971). *Discrepancy evaluation for education program improvement and assessment*. Berkeley, CA: McCutchan.

Rand, T. M., & Wexley, K. N. (1975). Demonstration of the effect, "Similar to me," in simulated employee interviews. *Psychological Reports, 36*: 535–544.

Reeser, C. (1975). Executive performance appraisal: The view from the top. *Personnel Journal, 54*(January): 42–46, 66–68.

Rendero, T. (1980). Consensus: Performance appraisal practices. *Personnel, 57*(6): 4–12.

Romberg, R. V. (1986). Performance appraisal 1: Risks and rewards. *Personnel, 63*(8): 20–26.

Ruderman, G. P. (1967). Employee merit rating. In H. B. Maynard (Ed.), *Handbook of business management*. New York: McGraw-Hill, pp. 11–144 to 11–156.

Schick, M. E. (1980). The "refined" performance evaluation monitoring system: Best of both worlds. *Personnel Journal, 59*(January): 47–50.

Schowengerdt, R. N. (1975). How reliable are merit rating techniques? *Personnel Journal, 54*(July): 390–392.

Schoderbek, P. P., & Reif, W. E. (1969). Introduction. In *Job enlargement: Key to improving performance*. Ann Arbor: University of Michigan, Bureau of Industrial Relations, pp. 7–25.

Schuster, J. R. (1985). How to control job evaluation inflation. *Personnel Administrator, 30*(6): 167–173.

Schwab, D. P., Heneman, H. G., III, & DeCotiis, T. A. (1975). Behavioral anchored rating scales: A review of the literature. *Personnel Psychology, 28*: 549–562.

Sergiovanni, T. J., & Starratt, R. J. (1979). *Supervision: Human perspective* (2nd ed.). New York: McGraw-Hill, pp. 98–130.

Shore, L. M., & Bloom, A. J. (1986). Developing employees through coaching and career management. *Personnel, 63*(8): 34–41.

Slusher, E. A. (1975). A systems look at performance appraisal. *Personnel Journal, 54*(February): 114–117.

Smith, P. C., & Kendall, L. M. (1963). Retranslation of expectations: An approach to the construction of unambiguous anchors for rating scales. *Journal of Applied Psychology, 47*(2): 149–155.

Snell, S. A., & Wexley, K. N. (1985). Poor performance diagnosis: Identifying the cause of poor performance. *Personnel Administration, 30*(4): 117–127.

Stedry, A. C., & Kay, E. (1966). The effects of goal difficulty on performance: A field experiment. *Behavioral Science, 11*: 459–470.

Sweeney, H. J., & Teel, K. S. (1979). A new look at promotion from within. *Personnel Journal, 58*(July): 531–535.

Teel, K. S. (1980). Performance appraisal: Current trends and persistent progress. *Personnel Journal, 59*(April): 296–301, 316.

Teel, K. S. (1986). Compensation: Are merit raises really based on merit? *Personnel Journal, 65*(March): 88–99.

Thornton, G. C., III. (1980). Psychometric properties of self-appraisal of job performance. *Personnel Psychology, 33*: 263–271.

Tiffin, J., & McCormick, E. J. (1962). Industrial merit ratings. In T. L. Whisler & S. F. Harper (Eds.), *Performance appraisal research and practices*. New York: Holt, Rinehart, & Winston, pp. 4–7.

Tjosvold, D. (1983). Managing peer relationships among subordinates. *Personnel, 60*(6): 13–22.

Torrence, W. D. (1975). Manpower planning and reduction in force: Competitive status, seniority, and EEOC compliance. *Personnel Journal, 54*(May): 287–289.

Tosi, H. L., & Carroll, S. (1970). Management by objective. *Personnel Administrator, 33*(3): 44–48.

Tosi, H. L., Rizzo, J. R. & Carroll, S. J. (1970). Setting goals in management by objective. *California Management Review, 12*(4): 70–78.

U. S. Equal Employment Opportunity Commission (EEOC). (1974). *Affirmative action and equal employment: A guidebook for employers* (Vol. 1). Washington, DC: EEOC.

Vogel, A. (1982). Employee surveys: The risks, the benefits. *Personnel, 59*(1): 65–70.

Wadsworth, G. W., Jr. (1962). Seniority and merit ratings in labor relations. In T. L. Whisler & S. F. Harper (Eds.), *Performance appraisal research and practices*. New York: Holt, Rinehart, & Winston, pp. 55–64.

Webb, D. R. (1972). The computer in personnel administration. In J. J. Famularo (Ed.), *Handbook of modern personnel administration*. New York: McGraw-Hill, pp. 79–1 to 79–13.

Wehrenberg, S. B. (1986). The vicious circle of training and organizational development. *Personnel Journal, 65*(July): 94–100.

Wells, R. G. (1982). Guidelines for effective and defensible performance appraisal. *Personnel Journal, 60*(October): 776–782.

Wexley, K. N., & Yukl, G. A. (1977). Measuring employee proficiency. In *Organizational behavior and personnel psychology*. Homewood, IL: Richard D. Irwin, Inc., pp. 197–228.

White, S. E., & Mitchell, T. R. (1979). Job enrichment versus social cues: A comparison and competitive test. *Journal of Applied Psychology, 64*(1): 1–9.

Wight, D. T. (1985). The split role in performance appraisal. *Personnel Administrator, 30*(5): 83–87.

Woltz, W. T. (1980). How to interview supervisor candidates from the ranks. *Personnel, 57*(5): 31–39.

Worthen, B. R., & Sanders, J. R. (1973). *Education evaluation: Theory and practice*. Worthington, OH: Charles A. Jones, pp. 22–44.

Yager, E. (1981). A critique of performance appraisal systems. *Personnel Journal*, *60*(February): 129–133.

Zedeck, S., & Cascio, W. F. (1982). Performance appraisal decisions as a function of rater training and purpose of the appraisal. *Journal of Applied Psychology*, *67*(6): 752–758.

Index

About the Author

JOE BAKER, JR., has a doctorate in Educational Leadership and more than 35 years of practical experience as a manager, supervisor, trainer, teacher, and counselor.